HOME-STYLE
TAIWANESE COOKING

HOME-STYLE TAIWANESE COOKING

Family Favourites

Classic Street Foods

Popular Snacks

Liv Wan

Marshall Cavendish Cuisine

Editor: Lydia Leong
Photographer: Chris Radley of Chris Radley Photography (chrisradleyphotography.com)
Illustrator: Liv Wan of Liv Wan Illustration (livwanillustration.com)

ISBN 978 981 4974 868

Published by Marshall Cavendish Cuisine
An imprint of Marshall Cavendish International

A member of the
Times Publishing Group

Other Marshall Cavendish Offices:
Marshall Cavendish Corporation, 800 Westchester Ave, Suite N-641, Rye Brook,
NY 10573, USA • Marshall Cavendish International (Thailand) Co Ltd, 253 Asoke,
16th Floor, Sukhumvit 21 Road, Klongtoey Nua, Wattana, Bangkok 10110, Thailand •
Marshall Cavendish (Malaysia) Sdn Bhd, Times Subang, Lot 46, Subang Hi-Tech
Industrial Park, Batu Tiga, 40000 Shah Alam, Selangor Darul Ehsan, Malaysia

Marshall Cavendish is a registered trademark of Times Publishing Limited

Printed in Singapore

DEDICATION

To everyone who helped us during the development of this book. Without your help, this book would not have been possible.

CONTENTS

POULTRY AND EGGS

Drunken Chicken 醉雞 60

Dragon Phoenix Legs 龍鳳腿 62

Fried Chicken with Sweet Potato Fries 鹽酥雞和炸地瓜 64

Deep-fried Chicken Legs Stuffed with Savoury Glutinous Rice 炸雞腿包油飯 66

Boiled Chicken with Spicy Ginger-garlic Dip 白斬雞 69

Three-cup Chicken 三杯雞 70

Oyster Omelette 蚵仔煎 72

Omelette with Preserved Radish 菜脯蛋 75

Soy Sauce Eggs 滷蛋 76

Steamed Egg with Seafood Sauce 海鮮蒸蛋 78

FISH AND SEAFOOD

Squid with Taiwanese Five-flavour Sauce 五味花枝 82

Stir-fried Squid with Celery 芹菜炒花枝 84

Stir-fried Oysters and Tofu with Black Bean Sauce 蔭鼓蚵仔豆腐 86

Steamed Prawns with Glass Noodles and Garlic Sauce 蒜蓉冬粉蒸蝦 88

Deep-fried Prawn Rolls 炸蝦捲 91

Stir-fried Mussels with Basil 塔香九孔 92

Steamed Halibut with Pickled Cordia 破布子蒸魚 94

Deep-fried Fish and Pork Rolls 炸雞卷 97

SOUPS

Ginger and Sesame Oil Chicken Soup 麻油雞 100

Mustard Green Chicken Soup 長年菜雞湯 102

Pickled Pineapple and Bitter Gourd Chicken Soup 鳳梨苦瓜雞湯 104

Pork Ball Soup 貢丸湯 107

White Radish and Pork Rib Soup 白蘿蔔排骨湯 108

White Radish and Fried Pork Rib Soup 排骨酥湯 111

Pork and Fish Dumpling Soup 肉羹湯 113

Salmon Tofu Miso Soup 鮭魚味噌湯 114

INTRODUCTION

Taiwanese cuisine is strongly influenced by the food of China and Japan, but has over time, developed its own unique styles and flavours. As such, you will find that some dishes and ingredients in Taiwan's rich cuisine originate from China or Japan, such as pork belly with garlic sauce or salmon miso soup, but yet, these dishes and ingredients are prepared and used in different ways, becoming distinctively Taiwanese.

For the Taiwanese, food is intimately intertwined with culture. Food is used to welcome and celebrate life, and to mourn the death of loved ones. Food is present at holidays and festivals and also when discussing business. Food represents leisure and relaxation, being key to the vibrant nightlife in Taiwan. The Taiwanese also have fun giving their dishes unusual names such as coffin bread, tiger bites pig and dragon phoenix leg among others, as well as taking part in food festivals such as the annual Taipei International Beef Noodle Soup Festival where chefs all over the country compete for the coveted title of World's Best Beef Noodle Soup.

It is no wonder that food has come to mean so much to me. I was born in Taiwan and my family business was running classic Taiwanese food restaurants. It was my grandmother who taught me about Taiwanese cooking and inspired me to study at one of the top food colleges in Taiwan.

I moved to the UK in 2007 and every time I thought of Taiwan, three things came to mind: my family, the weather and the food. While I could keep in touch with my family regularly and moan about the freezing temperatures in Edinburgh where I live, finding authentic Taiwanese food in the UK, at least in restaurants, was practically impossible. So, in 2009, I started my food blog: Egg Wan's Food Odyssey to share recipes with people from all over the world who have tasted and love Taiwanese cuisine, and with other Taiwanese who live abroad like me and miss the incredible food of Taiwan.

This book is a result of my food blog and my desire to share the authentic flavours of Taiwan with all who appreciate good food. Enjoy!

Liv Wan

ONE-DISH MEALS

MINCED PORK RICE 魯肉飯

Serves 7

This is one of my favourite Taiwanese dishes. It is available throughout Taiwan and it is also an incredibly popular night market dish. You will see this sold in almost every night market. This dish is easy to make and absolutely delicious. You can prepare a large batch and store it in the freezer for heating up whenever you feel like eating it.

800 g (1³/₄ lb) pork belly

Cooking oil, as needed

15 g (¹/₂ oz) garlic, peeled

30 g (1 oz) rock sugar

60 g (2¹/₄ oz) crisp-fried shallots

800 ml (26 fl oz) water

7 bowls cooked white rice

7 soy sauce eggs (page 76), halved

Seasoning

85 ml (2¹/₂ fl oz) light soy sauce

4 Tbsp thick soy sauce

¹/₂ Tbsp dark soy sauce

2 Tbsp rice wine

1 tsp Chinese five-spice powder

1. Clean the pork belly. Boil a large pot of water and blanch the pork belly briefly to remove any impurities. Drain and rinse immediately with cold water. Pat dry and cut into strips.

2. Heat ¹/₂ Tbsp oil in a wok over medium heat. Add the pork belly strips and garlic. Stir-fry until the pork belly is just golden brown.

3. Add the rock sugar and stir-fry for 3–5 minutes until the sugar is dissolved.

4. Add the crisp-fried shallots and stir-fry for 2–3 minutes. Transfer everything to a stockpot.

5. Add the water and seasoning. Bring to a boil, then simmer over low heat for 2 hours.

6. Dish out and serve with rice and soy sauce eggs, if desired.

NEW YEAR PORK FRIED RICE 臘肉炒飯

Serves 4

My name for the waxed pork used in this dish is New Year pork as it is traditionally only available for sale during the Chinese New Year. There is a shop in Taipei where my parents buy New Year pork. As they sell so much of it during the Chinese New Year period, they only open during that time and are closed for the rest of the year. Waxed pork can be considered the Taiwanese/Chinese equivalent of pancetta and one of our traditional ways of preparing it is to steam cook it with rice. This allows the juices from the pork to be soaked up by the rice, making it super delicious.

80 g (2⁴/₅ oz) peas

80 g (2⁴/₅ oz) carrot, peeled and cut into pea-size cubes

2 Tbsp cooking oil

200 g (7 oz) waxed pork, cut into small cubes

400 g (14¹/₃ oz) cooked white rice, chilled

30 g (1 oz) spring onion, finely chopped

15 g (¹/₂ oz) garlic, peeled and finely chopped

2 Tbsp light soy sauce

¹/₄ tsp ground white pepper

Scrambled Egg

3 large eggs

1 tsp light soy sauce

¹/₂ tsp sugar

1 Tbsp cooking oil

1. Prepare the scrambled egg. Beat the eggs with the soy sauce and sugar. Heat the oil in a wok over medium heat and add the beaten eggs. When the eggs are almost set, use a spatula to scramble it. Dish out and set aside.

2. Boil a small pot of water and cook the peas until tender. Drain and rinse with cold water. Drain again and set aside. Cook the carrots in the same way.

3. In a clean wok, heat the oil and add the waxed pork. Stir-fry for 3–5 minutes until fragrant.

4. Add the rice and stir-fry to mix. Press down on any lumps to break them up.

5. Add the scrambled egg, spring onion, garlic, peas and carrot. Stir-fry until heated through.

6. Season with soy sauce and pepper and mix well.

7. Dish out. Garnish as desired and serve.

Note: This recipe uses very little light soy sauce and salt as the waxed pork is often quite salty and will provide most of the flavour needed. If waxed pork is not available, pancetta or bacon lardons can be used as a substitute.

Waxed pork

SAVOURY GLUTINOUS RICE 油飯

Serves 4

There are different ways of preparing this dish and this is my version. I tend to season the mixture rather heavily before mixing it into the glutinous rice. Taste and adjust the seasoning before mixing it with the rice, as it will be difficult to adjust the flavour afterwards.

390 g (13³/₄ oz) glutinous rice

235 ml (7⁴/₅ fl oz) water

2 Tbsp dried prawns, soaked in hot water to soften

20 g (²/₃ oz) dried squid, soaked in hot water to soften

5 dried shiitake mushrooms, soaked in hot water to soften

1 Tbsp cooking oil

400 g (14¹/₃ oz) pork belly, thinly sliced

30 g (1 oz) crisp-fried shallots

90 ml (3 fl oz / ³/₈ cup) light soy sauce, or to taste

1 tsp Chinese five-spice powder

Seasoning

50 ml (1²/₃ fl oz) rice wine

1 Tbsp sugar

¹/₄ tsp ground white pepper

1. Place the glutinous rice and water in a rice cooker and cook according to the manufacturer's instructions.

2. Drain the dried prawns and set aside.

3. Drain the dried squid and slice it thinly. Set aside.

4. Squeeze the excess water from the shiitake mushrooms and reserve the soaking liquid. Slice the mushrooms thinly and set aside.

5. Heat the oil in a wok over medium heat. Add the dried prawns, squid and shiitake mushrooms and stir-fry for about 2 minutes.

6. Add the pork belly, crisp-fried shallots, soy sauce and five-spice powder and stir-fry for 3–4 minutes.

7. Add the seasoning and the liquid from soaking the shiitake mushrooms. Bring to a boil, then simmer over low heat for 25 minutes. Taste and adjust the seasoning as desired.

8. Add the contents of the wok to the cooked glutinous rice and mix evenly. Place in a steamer and steam for 10 minutes.

9. Dish out. Garnish as desired and serve immediately.

BEEF NOODLES 紅燒牛肉麵

Serves 5

This is often said to be the national dish of Taiwan as the Taiwanese simply love beef noodles. There is even an International Beef Noodle Festival held in Taiwan every year. There are many varieties of beef noodles in Taiwan and restaurants serving the dish will have their secret ingredients and recipes for their signature beef noodles, but the three main types of beef noodles are clear broth noodles, tomato broth beef noodles and red roasted or braised/stewed beef noodles such as the recipe below. When preparing beef noodles, choose a cut of beef with some fat as it will add to the flavour.

1 kg (2 lb 3 oz) beef flank or shin, with some fat

Cooking oil, as needed

30 g (1 oz) spring onion

30 g (1 oz) garlic

3 thin slices ginger

1 red chilli, or to taste

1 star anise

$1/2$ cinnamon stick

2 Tbsp chilli bean sauce

150 ml (5 fl oz) rice wine

100 ml ($3^1/2$ fl oz) light soy sauce

$1/2$ Tbsp dark soy sauce

1.25 litres (40 fl oz / 5 cups) water or stock (page 153)

2 slices licorice root (optional)

$1/2$ tsp salt

250 g (9 oz) carrots, peeled and cut into 2.5-cm (1-in) cubes

5 stalks bok choy or other green leafy vegetables

500 g (1 lb $1^1/2$ oz) dried wheat noodles

1. Boil a large pot of water and blanch the beef briefly to remove any impurities. Remove and rinse immediately with cold water. Cut into 1.5-cm ($3/4$-in) thick slices. Set aside.

2. Heat 1 Tbsp oil in a wok over medium heat. Add the spring onion, garlic, ginger, chilli, star anise and cinnamon and stir-fry until fragrant.

3. Add the chilli bean sauce and stir-fry for 10 seconds.

4. Add the beef and stir-fry for 2 minutes.

5. Add the rice wine and soy sauces and cook for 1 minute. Transfer everything to a stockpot.

6. Add the water or stock, liquorice root and salt. Bring to a boil, then simmer over low heat for about 2 hours until the beef is tender.

7. When the meat is almost ready, add the carrots and cook until soft. Blanch the bok choy briefly in the hot stock.

8. Boil a fresh pot of water and cook the noodles until tender. Divide the noodles among serving bowls and top with some carrot and bok choy. Ladle the beef and stock over.

9. Serve immediately.

STIR-FRIED SEAFOOD NOODLES
海鮮炒麵

Serves 4

If there's one thing Taiwan will never lack, it's seafood. Taiwan is a tropical island surrounded by the sea, providing access to some of the most delicious seafood imaginable. Prepared with fresh local seafood, this noodle dish is popular in Taiwanese night markets and restaurants. Traditionally, a type of noodle called alkaline noodle was used. This is similar to that used in home-made noodle salad (page 24), but egg noodles can also be used to make the dish easier and faster to cook at home.

300 g (11 oz) prawns, peeled and deveined

400 g (14^1/$_3$ oz) squid, cleaned, scored and cut into small pieces (page 82)

200 g (7 oz) cod fillet, cut into 2.5-cm (1-in) cubes

400 g (14^1/$_3$ oz) egg noodles

Cooking oil, as needed

20 g (^{2}/$_3$ oz) spring onion, cut into 3-cm (1^1/$_4$-in) lengths

1 tsp finely chopped ginger

80 g (2^4/$_5$ oz) onion, peeled and thinly sliced

200 g (7 oz) cabbage, cut into thin strips

100 g (3^1/$_2$ oz) carrot, peeled and cut into thin strips

Seasoning

1 Tbsp black vinegar

1 Tbsp rice wine

2 Tbsp light soy sauce

^{1}/$_4$ tsp ground white pepper

1 tsp sugar

1 tsp salt

1. Boil a pot of water and blanch the prawns, squid and fish. Remove and plunge immediately into cold water. Drain and set aside.

2. Boil a fresh pot of water and cook the egg noodles until tender. Drain and toss with some oil to prevent the noodles from sticking together. Set aside.

3. Heat 2 Tbsp oil in a wok over medium heat. Add the spring onion, ginger and onion and stir-fry until fragrant.

4. Add the cabbage and carrot and stir-fry for 2 minutes.

5. Add the prawns, squid, fish and noodles, and stir-fry for another 2 minutes.

6. Add the seasoning and stir-fry for 2 minutes until the sauce has been absorbed.

7. Dish out. Garnish as desired and serve immediately.

HOME-MADE NOODLE SALAD 涼麵

Serves 4–6

This noodle salad is a summer dish, but it is readily available throughout the year in Taiwan. Omit the chicken breast to make this dish vegetarian.

Noodles

425 g (15 oz) bread flour

1 tsp salt

215 ml (7^1/$_6$ fl oz) water

^{1}/$_2$ Tbsp lye water

Cooking oil for coating the noodles

Salad

2 chicken breasts

A pinch of salt

A pinch of ground white pepper

1 carrot, peeled and cut into thin strips

1 cucumber, cut into thin strips

Eggs

2 large eggs

A pinch of ground white pepper

^{1}/$_2$ tsp light soy sauce

Cooking oil, as needed

Sesame Dressing

140 g (5 oz) white sesame seeds

2 Tbsp vegetable oil or sunflower oil

1 tsp finely chopped garlic

100 ml (3^1/$_2$ fl oz) water

1 tsp rice vinegar

2 Tbsp light soy sauce

1 tsp salt

1 tsp sugar

1. Prepare the noodles. Place the bread flour and salt in a large mixing bowl. Make a well in the centre and add the water and lye water. Stir to combine, then knead into a soft dough. Flatten the dough and cut it into 4 parts.

2. Using a rolling pin, flatten each piece of dough out until it is thin enough to fit through a pasta maker, then pass it through the roller several times, changing to a finer setting each time. (For the pasta maker I have, 1 is the thickest setting and 9 is the thinnest. I started at setting number 1 and ended at 4.)

3. Feed the dough through the cutting blades in the pasta maker. Dust the noodles with flour to prevent them from sticking.

4. Boil a pot of water and cook the noodles for 2–3 minutes until the noodles are tender but still firm in the centre. Drain the noodles, then place into cold water to cool. Drain.

5. Mix the noodles with a little bit of oil to prevent the noodles from sticking. Set aside.

6. Prepare the salad. Season the chicken with salt and pepper, then roll each piece up in plastic wrap. Place in a steamer and steam for 15–20 minutes, until the chicken is cooked through. Let the chicken cool slightly before peeling off the plastic wrap. Cut into thin strips.

7. Prepare the eggs. Beat the eggs and season with the soy sauce and pepper. Heat some oil in a large frying pan over medium heat. Pour the beaten egg into the pan and tilt it around so the egg coats the base of the pan. Let it cook into a thin, crepe-like sheet. Remove the egg from the pan and let it cool slightly. Roll up the egg and cut into thin strips.

8. Prepare the sesame dressing. Heat a frying pan over medium heat. Add the white sesame seeds and toast until just golden brown. Remove and place immediately into a food processor with the oil. Process into a purée. Add the remaining ingredients for the dressing and process until smooth. Adjust to taste with salt and soy sauce.

9. Divide the noodles into serving bowls and top with chicken, carrot, cucumber and egg. Drizzle with sesame dressing. Mix and serve.

STIR-FRIED RICE NOODLES 炒米粉

Serves 4

This dish originates from Hsinchu County and it is the most popular rice noodle dish in Taiwan. Hsinchu is known as the windy city and it was the ideal place for the production of rice noodles as rice noodles were dried in the wind. In the olden days, almost every family living in Hsinchu was in some way involved in making rice noodles.

375 g (13¼ oz) dried rice noodles, soaked in water to soften

5 dried shiitake mushrooms, soaked in hot water to soften

1 Tbsp dried prawns, soaked in hot water to soften

2 Tbsp cooking oil

100 g (3½ oz) carrot, peeled and cut into thin strips

60 g (2¼ oz) onion, peeled and thinly sliced

350 g (12 oz) pork loin, cut into thin strips

2 Tbsp crisp-fried shallots

150 g (5⅓ oz) cabbage, shredded

Seasoning

500 ml (16 fl oz / 2 cups) stock (page 153)

100 ml (3½ fl oz) light soy sauce

1 Tbsp rice wine

½ tsp black vinegar

1 tsp sugar

¼ tsp ground white pepper

1. Drain the rice noodles and use a pair of scissors to cut the noodles into shorter lengths.

2. Squeeze the excess water from the shiitake mushrooms and reserve the soaking liquid. Slice the mushrooms thinly and set aside.

3. Heat the oil in a wok over medium heat. Add the dried prawns, mushrooms, carrot and onion and stir-fry for 2 minutes.

4. Add the pork and crisp-fried shallots and stir-fry for another 2 minutes.

5. Add the cabbage and stir-fry for 2–3 minutes.

6. Add the seasoning and the liquid from soaking the shiitake mushrooms. Bring to a boil, then simmer over low heat for 15–20 minutes.

7. Add the rice noodles and mix evenly. Stir-fry until the noodles are cooked and most of the liquid has been absorbed.

8. Dish out. Garnish as desired and serve.

SMOKED DUCK NOODLE SOUP 燻鴨麵

Serves 2

Smoked duck noodle soup is one of the most popular street foods in Hsinchu City, known as the technology capital of Taiwan. The traditional cooking method for this dish is complicated and I have used a simplified version which will allow you to make it easily at home. Whichever way you prepare this dish, it is a thoroughly delicious dish.

4 duck legs

Cooking oil, as needed

Sesame oil, as needed

200 g (7 oz) egg noodles

100 g (3½ oz) green vegetables of choice

A handful of coriander leaves

Marinade

1 Tbsp ground Sichuan pepper

1 Tbsp salt

2 Tbsp Shaoxing wine

Soup

30 g (1 oz) spring onion

3 slices ginger

½ cinnamon stick

1 star anise

1 litre (32 fl oz / 4 cups) water

3 Tbsp light soy sauce

1 Tbsp demerara sugar

1 piece dried tangerine peel

For Smoking the Duck

150 g (5⅓ oz) demerara sugar

2 Tbsp plain flour

30 g (1 oz) tea leaves

2 star anise

1. Marinate the duck legs with the ingredients for the marinade. Cover and set aside in the refrigerator for at least 1 hour.

2. Prepare the soup. Heat 2 Tbsp oil in a saucepan over medium heat. Add the spring onion, ginger, cinnamon and star anise and stir-fry until fragrant. Add the water, soy sauce, sugar and tangerine peel and bring to a boil.

3. Add the marinated duck legs and return to a boil. Lower the heat and simmer for 45 minutes. Remove the duck legs and set the soup aside.

4. Line a roasting pan with a sheet of aluminium foil and spread the ingredients for smoking the duck in the pan. Place a wire rack in the pan and place the duck legs on the rack, skin side down. Cover the pan with another sheet of aluminium foil.

5. Place the covered pan on the stove and turn the heat to medium. After 2–3 minutes, the ingredients should start smoking. Leave to smoke for 10 minutes.

6. Remove the duck legs from the pan and brush with some sesame oil.

7. Debone 2 duck legs and place the duck meat in the saucepan with the soup. Simmer over low heat for 1 hour.

8. Boil a pot of water and blanch the noodles and green vegetables. Divide into two bowls. Ladle some soup over and top with the duck legs and duck meat. Garnish with coriander leaves and serve.

SWORDFISH RICE NOODLE SOUP

旗魚米粉

Serves 2

In Taipei, there is a Taiwanese rice noodle soup stall that I really enjoy eating at, and it is called Swordfish Rice Noodle Soup. When I was living in Taipei, whenever my parents and I went out for a weekend brunch, I would almost always have a bowl of swordfish rice noodle soup from the stall.

250 g (9 oz) swordfish fillet, skinned and cut into 2.5-cm (1-in) cubes

200 g (7 oz) dried rice vermicelli, soaked in water to soften

1 Tbsp crisp-fried shallots

1 spring onion, cut into short lengths

A handful of coriander leaves

Stock

2 Tbsp cooking oil

2 slices ginger

30 g (1 oz) spring onion, cut into 3-cm (1¼-in) lengths

30 g (1 oz) shallots, peeled and sliced

2 litres (64 fl oz / 8 cups) water

50 g (1¾ oz) bonito flakes

Seasoning

Sesame oil, to taste

Salt, to taste

Ground white pepper, to taste

1. Prepare the stock. Heat the oil in a stockpot over medium heat. Add the ginger, spring onion and shallots and stir-fry until fragrant.

2. Add the water and bonito flakes. Bring to a boil, then simmer over low heat for 1 hour.

3. Strain the stock back into the stockpot and bring to a boil.

4. Poach the swordfish in the stock and drain. Set aside.

5. Drain the rice vermicelli and add to the stock to cook.

6. Add some sesame oil, salt, crisp-fried shallots and pepper to each serving bowl. Ladle some rice vermicelli and stock over, the top with swordfish. Garnish with spring onion and coriander. Serve immediately.

TAN TSAI NOODLES 擔仔麵

Serves 4

Tan Tsai Noodles is also known as Danzai Noodles. The story of these noodles began in 1895, with a fisherman named Hong. During the typhoon season or slack season, when it would be dangerous for fishermen to go out to sea, Hong had to find another way to make a living. He recalled a recipe he had learnt previously and made some changes to it with the ingredients he had on hand, coming up with this noodle dish. It became so popular, he decided to sell noodles full-time. He sold the noodles from street to street, carrying his cooking equipment and ingredients on shoulder poles. He then called the noodles "*tu hsian yueh tan tsai mian*", meaning slack season, shoulder pole noodles.

400 g (14^1/$_3$ oz) *tan tsai* noodles, Taiwan oil noodles or flat rice noodles

A handful of coriander leaves

Stock

6 prawns

2 Tbsp cooking oil

150 g (5^1/$_3$ oz) chicken bones

1.5 litres (48 fl oz / 6 cups) water

2 Tbsp bonito flakes

30 g (1 oz) spring onion, cut into 3-cm (1^1/$_4$-in) lengths

2 slices ginger

Meat Sauce

2 Tbsp cooking oil

400 g (14^1/$_3$ oz) minced fatty pork or pork belly, cut into strips

125 ml (4 fl oz / ^{1}/$_2$ cup) light soy sauce

1 Tbsp rice wine

^{1}/$_2$ Tbsp rock sugar

2 Tbsp crisp-fried shallots

^{1}/$_4$ tsp ground white pepper

1 tsp Chinese five-spice powder

625 ml (20 fl oz / 2^1/$_2$ cups) water

1. Prepare the stock. Peel the prawns and set them aside. Heat the oil in a wok over medium heat. Add the prawn shells and stir-fry until fragrant. Set aside.

2. Preheat the oven to 180°C (350°F) and roast the chicken bones until nicely browned.

3. Place the prawn shells and chicken bones in a stockpot and add the water. Bring to a boil, then simmer over low heat for 2 hours.

4. Prepare the meat sauce. Heat 2 Tbsp oil in a wok over medium heat. Add the pork and stir-fry until golden brown.

5. Add the light soy sauce, rice wine, rock sugar, crisp-fried shallots, pepper, five-spice powder and water. Bring to a boil, then simmer over low heat for about 1 hour until the sauce is reduced by half.

6. Boil a pot of water and poach the prawns. Drain and set aside. Add the noodles to the boiling water and cook until tender. Drain and place into 4 serving bowls.

7. Ladle some stock over the noodles, then top with the meat sauce and prawns. Garnish with coriander leaves and serve immediately.

TIGER BITES PIG 虎咬豬

Serves 8–10

This dish is known as tiger bite pig because it looks as if the bread is chewing on a big piece of juicy pork. Besides this, it also looks like a wallet, and is taken to mean "rich" or "having a lot of money". So let's make it at home, eat a lot of it and hope for a prosperous year ahead! In recent years, there have been many different fillings created for this dish, including deep-fried chicken fillets, cod fish fillets and even beef to replace the original stewed pork belly. You can almost consider this dish the equivalent of a Taiwanese hamburger and the recipe below is the classic way to make this dish.

Braised Pork Belly

700 g (1¹/₂ lb) pork belly, cut into 1.5-cm (³/₄-in) thick slices

4 Tbsp light soy sauce

1 tsp brown sugar

2 Tbsp cooking oil

2 spring onions, sliced

40 g (1¹/₃ oz) garlic, peeled

¹/₂ red chilli, sliced

625 ml (20 fl oz / 2¹/₂ cups) water

50 ml (1²/₃ fl oz) rice wine

1 tsp dark soy sauce

10 g (¹/₃ oz) rock sugar

1 Tbsp thick soy sauce

A pinch of ground white pepper

Steamed Buns

5 g (¹/₆ oz) dried yeast

1 tsp sugar

180 ml (6 fl oz / ³/₄ cup) water

100 g (3 ¹/₂ oz) plain flour

150 g (51/3 oz) bread flour

Cooking oil, as needed

Garnish

1 Tbsp peanut powder

Castor sugar, to taste

A handful of coriander leaves

1. Prepare the braised pork belly. Marinate the pork with 1 Tbsp soy sauce and brown sugar. Set aside for at least 30 minutes.

2. Heat 1 Tbsp oil in a wok over low heat. Add the pork and sear until golden brown on both sides. Remove and let cool.

3. Heat the remaining 1 Tbsp oil in a stockpot over medium heat. Add the spring onions, garlic and chilli and stir-fry until fragrant. Add the pork and the rest of the ingredients for the braised pork. Bring to a boil over high heat, then simmer over low heat for about 1¹/₂ hours until the pork is tender.

4. Meanwhile, prepare the steamed buns. Mix the yeast and sugar with the water until dissolved. Add both types of flour and knead into a smooth dough. Cover the dough with a clean damp cloth or a sheet of plastic wrap and set aside for 30–40 minutes for the dough to rise.

5. When the dough has risen, cut it into 70 g (2¹/₂ oz) portions. Form each portion into a ball. On a lightly floured work surface, flatten each ball into an oval using a rolling pin.

6. Brush some oil over the flattened dough and drape each piece over the rolling pin to set the shape of the dough.

7. Place the dough into a large steamer and steam over high heat for 8–10 minutes. When done, the buns should spring back when lightly pressed with a finger.

8. Mix the peanut powder with some sugar. To assemble the buns, place 1–2 slices of braised pork into each bun. Garnish with the sweetened peanut powder and coriander leaves. Serve immediately.

 Note: For the garnishing, the traditional ratio of peanut powder to sugar is 4:1. For example, 100 g (3¹/₂ oz) peanut powder is usually mixed with 25 g (⁴/₅ oz) sugar. However, you can adjust the proportion according to your taste.

SALAD BOAT SANDWICHES 沙拉船三明治

Makes 14–15 sandwiches

This sandwich originates from Keelung Night Market but it has become so popular, it can be found in almost any night market in Taiwan. This dish got its name from its shape as it resembles a boat. Salad boat sandwiches are typically served with Taiwanese-style sweet mayonnaise, cucumber, tomato, ham and soy eggs, but you can fill the bread rolls with other ingredients as desired.

Bread Rolls

350 g (12 oz) bread flour

60 g (2¼ oz) plain flour

1 Tbsp milk powder

50 g (1¾ oz) castor sugar

1 tsp salt

1 egg

14 g (½ oz) dried yeast

180 ml (6 fl oz / ¾ cup) water

50 g (1¾ oz) unsalted butter, softened at room temperature

200 g (7 oz) breadcrumbs

1 litre (32 fl oz / 4 cups) vegetable oil or sunflower oil

Taiwanese-style Sweet Mayonnaise

1 tsp salt

90 g (3¼ oz) castor sugar

50 ml (1¾ fl oz) water

30 g (1 oz) potato starch or cornflour

4 tsp rice vinegar

2 eggs

400 ml (13½ fl oz) vegetable oil or sunflower oil

Filling (Optional)

1 cucumber, sliced

4–5 tomatoes, cut into wedges or sliced

14–15 slices of ham

Soy sauce eggs, sliced (page 76)

1. Prepare the bread rolls. Place both types of flour, milk powder, sugar, salt, and egg into a mixing bowl. Stir the yeast into the water until dissolved, then add to the mixing bowl. Knead the mixture for 5–10 minutes until the dough is smooth. Add the butter and mix evenly.

2. Cover the dough with a clean damp cloth or a sheet of plastic wrap. Set aside for 1–1½ hours for the dough to rise. The dough should double in size.

3. Divide the dough into 14–15 portions, each weighing about 60 g (2¼ oz). Roll each portion of dough into a ball. Press a rolling pin into a ball of dough and flatten the centre portion of the dough.

4. Using your fingers, roll up the flattened dough so it is slightly tapered at either end.

5. Dip the dough into some cold water, then coat it with breadcrumbs. Place on a tray. Repeat with the remaining balls of dough. Cover the coated dough with plastic wrap and set aside for 30–40 minutes for the dough to rise.

6. Heat the oil in a wok over high heat. Lower 2–3 rolls into the oil and deep-fry for 3–5 minutes until the rolls are golden brown. Remove and drain well. Repeat until all the rolls are done.

7. Prepare the mayonnaise. Place the salt, sugar, water, potato starch or cornflour and rice vinegar into a small saucepan. Cook over low heat, stirring constantly, until the mixture turns into a sticky, translucent paste. Remove from heat.

8. Lightly beat the eggs and gradually add the cooked mixture to the eggs, whisking until it takes on a creamy, buttery colour. Gradually add the oil, whisking all the time. (The oil will alter the viscosity of the mayonnaise and you can adjust the amount of oil added to your preference. I typically use about 400 ml / 13½ fl oz oil.)

9. Slit the rolls and spread with some mayonnaise. Fill with cucumber, tomato, ham and soy eggs or as desired.

3a

3b

4

5a

5b

MEAT

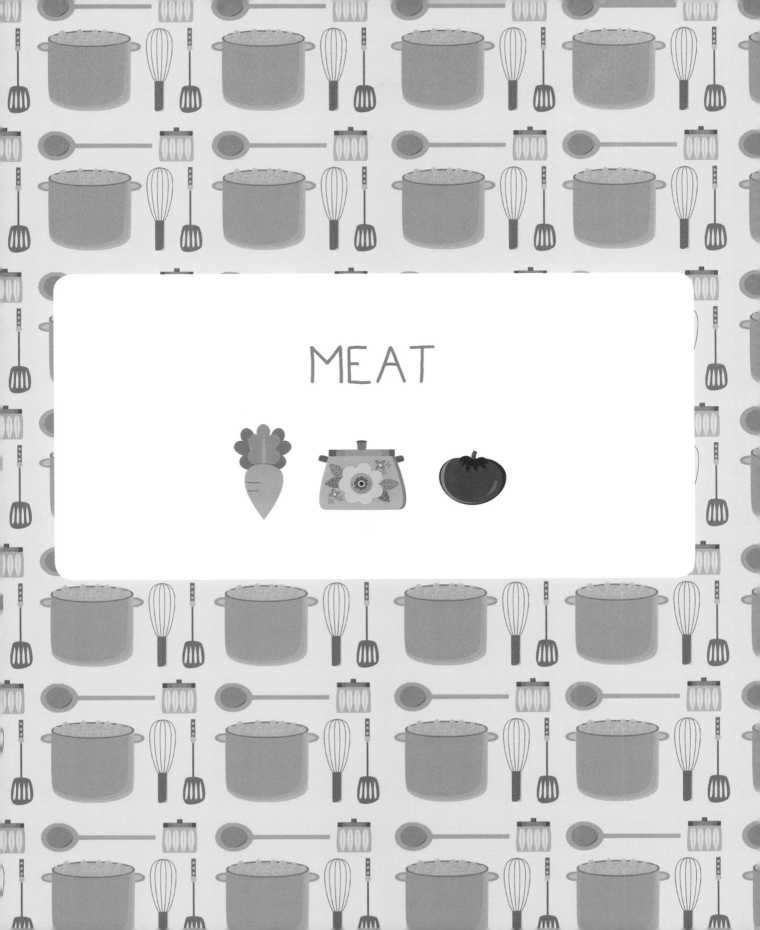

STEAMED MINCED PORK WITH SALTED EGG 鹽蛋蒸肉餅

Serves 3

This is another dish that I just have to eat when I am back in Taipei. Use fatty minced pork (at least 40% pork fat) or the texture of the final dish will be dry and tough. One either loves or hates salted eggs, but these preserved duck eggs with their salty aroma, really add to the flavour of this dish.

370 g (13 oz) fatty minced pork

1 tsp finely chopped garlic

1/4 tsp finely chopped ginger

55 g (2 oz) pickled melon, roughly chopped

1 Tbsp juices from pickled melon

3 salted eggs

Seasoning

1 tsp rice wine

1 Tbsp light soy sauce

1 tsp sugar

1. Line a loaf tin measuring 20 x 9 x 6 cm (7³/₄ x 3½ x 2¹/₄ in) with a sheet of baking paper.

2. Place all the ingredients, except the salted eggs, and seasoning in a bowl and mix evenly.

3. Pour the mixture into the loaf tin and use a spoon to compact it and flatten the top of the mixture.

4. Pour the egg whites from the salted eggs over the top of the mixture, then gently press the egg yolks into the mixture.

5. Steam over medium heat for 20–30 minutes until the meat is well done.

6. Unmould and serve immediately.

BOILED PORK BELLY WITH GARLIC SAUCE 蒜泥白肉

Serves 4

This dish originates from Sichuan in China, but it has become really popular in Taiwan where it is served cold during the hot summer months. There are many different ways to make the garlic sauce and this recipe belongs to my grandfather. He is originally from Sichuan and he used to cook this dish often when I was young. You can adjust the seasoning for this dish to suit your personal preference.

1.25 litres (40 fl oz / 5 cups) water

1 Tbsp rice wine

1 tsp salt

1 star anise

2 cardamom pods

30 g (1 oz) spring onion

2 knobs ginger, each about 2.5 cm (1 in)

1 kg (2 lb 3 oz) pork belly

1 cucumber, thinly sliced

1 Tbsp roasted crushed peanuts (optional)

Garlic Sauce

4 Tbsp light soy sauce

1 tsp sugar

$1/2$ tsp rice vinegar

1 tsp black vinegar

30 g (1 oz) garlic, peeled and finely chopped

1. Place the water, rice wine, salt, star anise, cardamom pods, spring onion and ginger into a stockpot. Bring to a boil over high heat, then lower the heat and simmer for 30 minutes.

2. Add the pork belly and bring to a boil. Lower the heat and simmer for about 1 hour until the pork is done. Test by piercing the pork with chopsticks. The chopsticks should go through the meat easily. Set aside to cool.

3. Place all the ingredients for the garlic sauce in a bowl. Add 2 Tbsp of stock from the stockpot and mix well. Set aside for at least 30 minutes.

4. Using a sharp knife, slice the cooled pork into 3-mm ($1/8$-in) thick slices.

5. Arrange the pork on a serving plate with the cucumbers. Garnish with crushed peanuts if desired. Serve with the garlic sauce.

BRAISED PORK BELLY WITH DRIED BAMBOO SHOOT 煙肉筍絲

Serves 4

This is a classic Taiwanese dish. It takes a long time to cook, but if you have the patience, you will be rewarded with an extremely delicious dish.

1.5 kg (3 lb 4¹/₂ oz) pork belly,
    cut into 2-cm (³/₄-in) thick slices

2 Tbsp light soy sauce

1 Tbsp brown sugar

250 g (9 oz) dried bamboo shoot,
    soaked in warm water for
    15 minutes

500 ml (16 fl oz / 2 cups) stock
    (page 153)

¹/₂ tsp salt

¹/₄ tsp ground white pepper

Cooking oil, as needed

2 spring onions, sliced

70 g (2¹/₂ oz) garlic, peeled

1 red chilli, sliced

900 ml (30 fl oz) water

A handful of coriander leaves

Seasoning

100 ml (3¹/₂ fl oz) rice wine

150 ml (5 fl oz) light soy sauce

2 Tbsp thick soy sauce

1 Tbsp dark soy sauce

30 g (1 oz) rock sugar

A pinch of ground white pepper

1. Marinate the pork belly with the light soy sauce and brown sugar. Set aside for 30 minutes.

2. Drain the dried bamboo shoot. Place into a small pot with the stock, salt and pepper. Bring to a boil, then simmer over low heat for 1 hour.

3. Heat 1 Tbsp oil in a wok over medium heat. Add the pork belly and stir-fry until golden brown. Dish out and set aside.

4. Heat 1 Tbsp oil in a stockpot. Add the spring onions, garlic and chilli and stir-fry until fragrant.

5. Add the browned pork belly and water, followed by the seasoning. Bring to a boil, then simmer over low heat for 2 hours.

6. Arrange the bamboo shoot on a serving plate. Top with the pork belly and drizzle with sauce. Garnish with coriander and serve.

BRAISED PORK HOCK 滷豬腳

Serves 5

Pork hock is a favourite with the Taiwanese, with the added benefit of the collagen being good for the skin. It is also widely believed that pork hock stewed with peanuts will help lactating mothers increase their milk supply. I tried it once after I gave birth, but it did not work for me, as I did not consume it regularly. Many Taiwanese swear by it though.

2 kg (4 lb 6 oz) pork hock

Cooking oil, as needed

30 g (1 oz) spring onion, cut into 3-cm (1¼ -in) lengths

2 knobs ginger, each about 2.5 cm (1 in), peeled

30 g (1 oz) garlic, peeled

1 red chilli

2 litres (64 fl oz / 8 cups) water

Seasoning

100 ml (3½ fl oz) rice wine

150 ml (5 fl oz) light soy sauce

1 Tbsp dark soy sauce

3 Tbsp thick soy sauce

30 g (1 oz) rock sugar

¼ tsp ground white pepper

1 star anise

1. Clean the pork hock. Boil a large pot of water and blanch the pork hock briefly to remove any impurities. Drain and rinse immediately with cold water. Pat dry and set aside.

2. Heat a little oil in a wok over low heat. Add the pork hock and cook until the skin turns a light golden colour. Remove and set aside.

3. Heat a little oil in a stockpot over medium heat. Add the spring onion, ginger, garlic and chilli and stir-fry until fragrant.

4. Add the pork hock and stir-fry for 1 minute.

5. Add the water and seasoning. Bring to a boil, then simmer over low heat for about 2½ hours until the pork hock is cooked through and tender.

6. Garnish as desired and serve.

 Note: Dry the pork hock before frying to prevent the oil from splattering. If the oil splatters, it might burn your skin.

DEEP-FRIED RED VINASSE PORK 紅糟肉

Serves 4–6

This deep-fried pork is commonly available in the food markets of Taiwan. Red vinasse refers to the lees of Shaoxing rice wine. The long marinating time ensures that the pork will be well-flavoured with a mouthwatering aroma of the vinasse. Incidentally, my husband doesn't like his food to taste of alcohol, but he absolutely loves this dish.

700 g (1¹/₂ lb) pork belly, cut into long strips
¹/₄ tsp finely chopped ginger
300 g (11 oz) sweet potato flour
1 litre (32 fl oz / 4 cups) cooking oil

Seasoning
4 Tbsp red vinasse (red wine lees)
1 Tbsp light soy sauce
1 Tbsp rice wine
1 tsp sugar

1. This dish must be prepared a day in advance.

2. Place the pork belly in a deep dish with the ginger and seasoning. Mix well. Cover and leave to marinate for at least 12 hours in the refrigerator.

3. Coat the marinated pork belly with the sweet potato flour and leave for 10 minutes.

4. Heat the oil in a wok to 180°C (350°F). Lower the pork belly into the hot oil and cook for 1 minute.

5. Turn off the heat and let the pork belly sit in the hot oil for 2 minutes.

6. Reheat the oil over low heat and cook until the pork belly is golden brown.

7. Remove and drain well. Slice and serve.

 Note: This method of cooking the pork, by heating up the oil, then turning off the heat and cooking over low heat will ensure that the meat is cooked from the inside out.

FRIED PORK CHOPS 炸排骨

Serves 4

This is a simple and quick recipe for the all-time favourite dish of pork chops. I usually marinade a large quantity of pork chops and store them in freezer bags in the freezer, then defrost and cook the marinated pork chops whenever I need to fix a meal quickly. This dish is ideal for busy people.

4 pork chops

1 Tbsp finely chopped spring onion

1 Tbsp finely chopped garlic

60 g (2¼ oz) plain flour

60 g (2¼ oz) sweet potato starch

1½ Tbsp water

1 egg white

1 litre (32 fl oz / 4 cups) cooking oil

Seasoning

3 Tbsp light soy sauce

½ tsp salt

2 tsp sugar

2 Tbsp rice wine

1 tsp Chinese five-spice powder

½ tsp ground black pepper

1. Using a meat mallet, pound the pork chops on both sides to tenderise it.

2. Place the pork chops in a deep dish and add the spring onion, garlic, flour, sweet potato starch, water and egg white. Mix well. Add the seasoning and mix again. Cover the dish and set aside in the refrigerator for at least 1 hour.

3. Before cooking, knead the pork chops for about 30 seconds. This will ensure that the pork chops absorb the marinade.

4. Heat the oil in a wok over medium heat to about 150°C (300°F). Lower the pork chops into the hot oil and deep-fry until the pork chops are nearly done. Remove the pork chops and set aside.

5. Increase to high heat and bring the temperature of the oil to about 180°C (350°F). Lower the pork chops into the hot oil and continue to deep-fry until well done and crisp. Drain well and serve.

STIR-FRIED LAMB WITH WATER SPINACH AND BBQ SAUCE 沙茶羊肉

Serves 4

You can find this dish almost anywhere in Taiwan, from restaurants to road side stalls and the night markets. It is also a dish popularly prepared at home. As a variation to this recipe, you can replace the lamb with beef or pork.

250 g (9 oz) thinly sliced lamb

1 Tbsp cooking oil

15 g (¹/₂ oz) garlic, peeled and finely chopped

15 g (¹/₂ oz) red chilli, finely sliced

250 g (9 oz) water spinach, rinsed and cut into 3-cm (1¹/₄-in) lengths

¹/₂ tsp potato starch or cornflour, mixed with 1 Tbsp water

Marinade

2 Tbsp light soy sauce

1 tsp sugar

¹/₂ tsp potato starch or cornflour

Seasoning

¹/₄ tsp dark soy sauce

1 tsp rice wine

¹/₂ tsp salt

¹/₂ tsp potato starch or cornflour

1 Tbsp water

1 Tbsp Chinese BBQ sauce

1. Place the lamb and the marinade in a bowl and mix well. Set aside for 15 minutes.

2. Combine the ingredients for the seasoning in another bowl and set aside.

3. Heat the oil in a wok over high heat. Add the lamb and stir-fry briefly.

4. Add the garlic and chilli and stir-fry for about 30 seconds.

5. Add the seasoning and stir-fry for a few minutes.

6. Add the water spinach and stir-fry until the leaves are wilted and the stems are just tender.

7. Add the potato starch or cornflour slurry and cook for 30 seconds.

8. Dish out and serve.

 Note: The thinly-sliced lamb called for in this recipe is typically used when making Taiwanese hotpot. It can be found in the frozen meat section in supermarkets.

STIR-FRIED MINCED BEEF WITH CORIANDER AND CHILLI 香菜炒牛肉末

Serves 3

Coriander is also known as Chinese parsley and Taiwanese cooks use a lot of coriander in their cooking. This green leafy herb has a strong fragrance which contributes to enhancing the flavour of dishes it is used in.

80 g (2⁴/₅ oz) coriander leaves

200 g (7 oz) minced beef

Cooking oil, as needed

10 g (^{1}/₃ oz) garlic, peeled and finely chopped

10 g (^{1}/₃ oz) red chilli, sliced

A pinch of salt

1 spring onion, sliced

Marinade

2 Tbsp light soy sauce

1 tsp brown sugar

1 tsp sesame oil

A pinch of ground black pepper

1 tsp Shaoxing wine

1. Rinse the coriander and pluck the leaves, leaving the stalks. Use the leaves for another dish. Chop the stalks.

2. Place the beef and the marinade in a bowl and mix well. Set aside for at least 30 minutes.

3. Heat 1 Tbsp oil in a wok over high heat. When the oil is smoking. Add the beef and stir-fry until browned. Dish out and set aside.

4. Heat 1 Tbsp oil in the wok over medium heat. Add the garlic and chilli and stir-fry until fragrant.

5. Add the coriander stalks and stir-fry for 10 seconds. Season with salt and increase to high heat. Add the beef and stir-fry for 1 minute.

6. Dish out. Garnish with spring onion and serve immediately.

STIR-FRIED BEEF WITH TAIWANESE-STYLE KIMCHI
台式泡菜炒牛肉

Serves 3

While writing this book, I recalled many dishes, but it has been a few years since I lived in Taiwan and my memory of the dishes had become a little vague. I spoke to my father to refresh my memory and he reminded me of this dish. This is a dish that everyone in my family loves. Those who do not normally eat cabbage also love this dish. Taiwanese-style kimchi is both sweet and sour, and the vegetables are crunchy. Complimented with soft and tender beef, this dish is rich in texture and has a refreshing flavour.

200 g (7 oz) sirloin steak, thinly sliced

1 tsp potato starch or cornflour

1 tsp sugar

1½ Tbsp light soy sauce

1 tsp rice wine

1 Tbsp cooking oil

1 tsp finely chopped garlic

150 g (5⅓ oz) Taiwanese-style kimchi (page 126)

1. Season the beef with the potato starch or cornflour, sugar, light soy sauce and rice wine. Set aside for at least 15 minutes.

2. Heat the oil in a wok over medium heat. Add the garlic and stir-fry for 10 seconds.

3. Add the beef and stir-fry for 1 minute.

4. Add the kimchi and stir-fry for 2–3 minutes.

5. Dish out. Garnish as desired and serve immediately.

POULTRY AND EGGS

UTENSILS

DRUNKEN CHICKEN 醉雞

Serves 3

As a child, I always imagined that this dish of drunken chicken was prepared by feeding the chicken a bottle of rice wine before it was cooked. I thought that it would make the meat taste of alcohol. How wrong I was! I love the taste of drunken chicken even though I am not a big fan of food that tastes of alcohol. Classic drunken chicken uses Shaoxing rice wine which has a strong but special flavour.

2 chicken legs, including drumsticks and thighs, deboned

1 tsp salt

Marinade

250 ml (8 fl oz / 1 cup) chicken stock (page 153)

250 ml (8 fl oz / 1 cup) water

2 spring onions, cut into 3-cm (1¼-in) lengths

2 thin slices ginger

1 Tbsp Chinese wolfberries

1 thin slice Chinese angelica root

2 thin slices licorice root

1 tsp sugar

200 ml (7 fl oz) Shaoxing wine

1. This dish must be prepared a day in advance.

2. Rub the chicken legs with the salt and set aside for 20 minutes.

3. Wrap the chicken tightly with several layers of plastic wrap, then twist the ends to seal. Set aside.

4. Prepare the marinade. Place the chicken stock, water, spring onions, ginger, wolfberries, angelica root, liquorice root and sugar in a small saucepan. Bring to a boil, then simmer over low heat for 20 minutes. Set aside to cool.

5. When the marinade is cool, stir in the Shaoxing wine.

6. Steam the wrapped chicken for about 20 minutes until the chicken changes colour and is cooked.

7. Remove the plastic wrap and place the chicken into the marinade. Cover and leave to soak for at least 12 hours in the refrigerator. Slice and serve chilled.

3a

3b

3c

DRAGON PHOENIX LEGS 龍鳳腿

Makes 10–12 pieces

This night market snack originates from the small fishing villages that surround the north coast of Taiwan. One of the stories behind this dish tells of how the poor people had to find ways to feed their families and so they came up with this dish, adding fish, pork and vegetables to make these 'chicken legs'. The mixture of fish and chicken gave this dish its name.

60 g (2¼ oz) spring greens, sliced

15 g (½ oz) spring onion, chopped

60 g (2¼ oz) carrot, peeled and grated

A pinch of salt

200 g (7 oz) minced fatty pork

10 g (⅓ oz) garlic, peeled and chopped

40 g (1⅓ oz) onion, peeled and chopped

12 sheets dried tofu skin, each 25 x 8-cm (10 x 3-in)

2 Tbsp plain flour, mixed with 3 Tbsp water

1 litre (32 fl oz / 4 cups) cooking oil

12 wooden skewers

Sweet chilli sauce

Fish Paste

600 g (1 lb 5⅓ oz) white fish meat, such as cod or haddock

1 tsp roughly chopped ginger

50 g (1¾ oz) cornflour

1½ tsp salt

1 tsp sugar

70 g (2½ oz) ice cubes

50 g (1¾ oz) cold water

Seasoning

3 Tbsp light soy sauce

1½ Tbsp castor sugar

¼ tsp ground white pepper

¼ tsp Chinese five-spice powder

1. Prepare the fish paste. Freeze the fish until it is hard but still soft enough to cut through with a knife. Cut the fish into small cubes. Using a food processor, blend the fish with the ginger until the mixture is smooth. Transfer to a large mixing bowl.

2. In a small bowl, mix the cornflour with the salt, sugar, ice and cold water. Mix until smooth. Add to the fish paste and mix well. Using clean hands, gather the fish paste and throw it back into the mixing bowl. Do this 20–30 times until the fish paste gains some viscidity. Set aside until needed.

3. Boil a pot of water and blanch the spring greens briefly. Remove and plunge into cold water to cool. Drain and squeeze out any excess water. Season the spring onion and carrot with a pinch of salt. Leave for 20 minutes, then squeeze out any excess water.

4. Prepare the filling. Measure out 200 g (7 oz) fish paste and place in a large bowl with the minced pork, garlic, onion, spring greens, spring onion and carrot. Add the seasoning and mix well. Divide the filling into 12 equal portions.

5. Wipe a sheet of dried tofu skin with a clean damp cloth, then spoon a portion of filling onto it. Wrap the tofu skin over the filling and shape it into a thick cylinder. Seal the edges of the tofu skin with the flour and water mixture. Repeat to make 12 rolls. Insert a wooden skewer into one end of each roll.

6. Heat the oil in a wok to 180°C (350°F). Lower 2–3 rolls into the hot oil and turn off the heat. Let the rolls sit in the hot oil for 1 minute. Reheat the oil over low heat and cook for 3–5 minutes until the rolls are golden brown. Remove and drain well. Repeat to cook the rest of the rolls.

7. Serve the dragon phoenix legs with sweet chilli sauce.

 Note: This method of frying food, by heating up the oil, then turning off the heat and cooking over low heat will ensure that the filling is thoroughly cooked without burning the skin.

FRIED CHICKEN WITH SWEET POTATO FRIES 鹽酥雞和炸地瓜

Serves 4

This is one of my favourite Taiwanese street foods and thus one of my favourite things to cook at home. You can use chicken thigh fillets or chicken breast for this dish. The basil gives extra flavour while lightening the dish, but it is optional. Chopped garlic is sometimes added to this dish for another dimension of flavour.

8 chicken thigh or breast fillets, cut into 2.5-cm (1-in) cubes

2 thin slices ginger, peeled and finely chopped

1 spring onion, finely chopped

150 g (5^1/$_3$ oz) sweet potato flour

30 g (1 oz) basil

1 litre (32 fl oz / 4 cups) cooking oil

Sweet chilli sauce

Sweet Potato Fries

2 Tbsp sweet potato flour

2–3 Tbsp water

2 medium sweet potatoes, peeled and cut into thin strips

Seasoning

3 Tbsp light soy sauce

1 tsp salt

1 tsp sugar

^{1}/$_2$ tsp ground black pepper

1 tsp Chinese five-spice powder

1. Mix the chicken with the ginger, spring onion and seasoning. Mix well and leave to marinate for at least 1 hour.

2. Coat the marinated chicken with some sweet potato flour. Set aside for 10 minutes.

3. Rinse the basil and pluck the leaves. Discard the stems.

4. Prepare the sweet potato fries. In a large bowl, mix the sweet potato flour with the water. Stir to mix evenly. Coat the sweet potato strips evenly with the mixture. Set aside.

5. Heat the oil in a wok to 180°C (350°F) and deep-fry the chicken until golden brown. When the chicken is nearly cooked, add the basil leaves. Be careful as the oil may splatter. Remove and set aside to drain.

6. Reheat the oil and deep-fry the sweet potato strips. Drain well.

7. Serve the chicken and sweet potato fries immediately with sweet chilli sauce on the side.

DEEP-FRIED CHICKEN LEGS STUFFED WITH SAVOURY GLUTINOUS RICE

炸雞腿包油飯

Serves 3

Even though the name of this dish gives the impression that it is deep-fried, this dish isn't entirely deep-fried. The chicken legs are first steamed to shape and cook the rolls, and it is only deep-fried it give it a crisp and golden finish.

3 chicken legs, including drumsticks and thighs

1 tsp salt

1/4 tsp ground black pepper

1 tsp rice wine

150 g (5¹/₃ oz) savoury glutinous rice (page 18)

1 litre (32 fl oz / 4 cups) cooking oil

Cornflour, as needed

Sweet chilli sauce or ketchup

1. Debone the chicken legs. Place a chicken leg on a chopping board with the exposed bone facing up. Using a sharp knife, cut the meat along the line of the bone from end to end.

2. Working down the side of the bone, use the knife to separate the meat from the bone. Get your fingers around the bone to loosen the meat. Cut around each end of the bone to free the meat from the bone.

3. Marinade the deboned chicken legs with the salt, pepper and rice wine.

4. Place a sheet of plastic wrap on a chopping board and spread a filleted chicken leg out on it, skin-side down. Spoon a third of the savoury glutinous rice onto it and roll the fillet up to enclose the rice. Wrap the roll with the plastic wrap. Repeat to make another 2 rolls.

5. Place the rolls in a steamer and steam for about 15 minutes. Leave to cool before removing the plastic wrap.

6. Heat the oil in a wok to 180°C (350°F). Coat the chicken rolls with cornflour and lower 1–2 rolls into the hot oil. Cook until the rolls are golden brown. Remove and drain well. Repeat to cook the other rolls.

7. Slice the rolls thickly and serve with sweet chilli sauce or ketchup.

BOILED CHICKEN WITH SPICY GINGER-GARLIC DIP 白斬雞

Serves 4

With this dish, the chicken is blanched in boiling water, then refreshed in cold water, and this process is repeated three to four times. This ensures that the chicken skin is firm without being too greasy and the meat remains succulent. This dish is extremely popular during the summer months in Taiwan.

2 litres (64 fl oz / 8 cups) water

30 g (1 oz) spring onion

30 g (1 oz) ginger, peeled and thinly sliced

1 star anise

1 tsp Sichuan peppercorns

300 g (11 oz) ice cubes

Cold water, as needed

1 medium-size chicken

2 Tbsp rice wine

1¹/₂ Tbsp salt

Dip

¹/₂ tsp finely chopped ginger

1 tsp finely chopped garlic

1 red chilli, finely chopped

2 Tbsp thick soy sauce

1 tsp salt

¹/₂ tsp sugar

¹/₄ tsp sesame oil

1¹/₂ Tbsp stock from boiling chicken

1. Place the water, spring onion, ginger, star anise and Sichuan peppercorns into a stockpot large enough to hold all the ingredients. Bring to a boil, then simmer over low heat for 30 minutes.

2. Fill a container or bowl large enough to hold the chicken with the ice, then half-fill it with cold water.

3. Lower the chicken into the stockpot and leave for 30 seconds. Remove the chicken and soak it in the iced water. Repeat this step 3–4 times, then drain the chicken and set aside.

4. Bring the water in the stockpot to a boil and add the chicken. Cook over medium heat for 30 minutes, then turn off the heat. Cover the pot and leave for 30 minutes.

5. Mix the ingredients for the dip evenly and let sit for at least 30 minutes.

6. Mix the rice wine with the salt.

7. Remove the chicken from the stockpot and rub well with the rice wine and salt mixture. Leave the chicken to cool completely.

8. Slice the chicken and serve with the dip.

 Note: If desired, chicken legs can be used in place of a whole chicken when preparing this dish.

THREE-CUP CHICKEN 三杯雞

Serves 4

The first time I heard about this dish, I thought it was a Taiwanese dish. But after doing some research, I discovered that originated from China. Wen Tiansiang was the Duke of Xinguo and he is known in Chinese history for his loyalty to the Song Dynasty. He refused Khubilai Khan's demand for the Song forces to surrender to the Khan invasion and suffered for four years in a military prison before he was executed. He wrote many poems in prison and one of the most well known lines from one of his poems goes "None since the advent of time have escaped death, may my loyalty forever illuminate the annuals of history." This dish was prepared by a kind prison warden who was also from Wen's home town in Jiangxi. He made this dish with limited ingredients, one cup of sweet rice wine, one cup of soy sauce and one cup of lard, to stew the chicken for Wen before his execution. In Taiwan, the recipe for this dish has evolved into one cup of rice wine, one cup of soy sauce and one cup of dark sesame oil. The aroma of this dish is just divine and it tastes wonderful as well.

2–3 Tbsp dark sesame oil

6 slices ginger

5 chicken legs, including drumsticks and thighs, deboned and cut into bite-size pieces

10 cloves garlic, peeled

1 red chilli, sliced

A handful of basil

Seasoning

90 ml (3 fl oz / $3/8$ cup) dark sesame oil

90 ml (3 fl oz / $3/8$ cup) light soy sauce

90 ml (3 fl oz / $3/8$ cup) rice wine

2 tsp sugar

$1/4$ tsp salt

1. Heat the dark sesame oil in a wok over medium heat. Add the ginger and stir-fry until the ginger is dry.

2. Add the chicken legs and stir-fry it until the chicken changes colour and is cooked.

3. Add the garlic, chilli and seasoning. Stir-fry to mix, then cover the wok and simmer over low heat for 15–20 minutes until the mixture is dry.

4. Add the basil and stir-fry lightly. Dish out and serve.

OYSTER OMELETTE 蚵仔煎

Serves 4

According to a Taiwanese legend, when the Dutch took control of Anping in Tainan City in the 17th century, the military leader, Zheng Cheng-gong (Koxinga) and his army fought the Dutch and defeated them. In anger, the Dutch army hid the food provisions, with the aim of starving Zheng's army. Undeterred by this, Zheng's army gathered oysters, mixed them with sweet potato starch and cooked them into dough-wrapped patties for food. This dish is now a popular snack throughout Taiwan.

4 Tbsp cooking oil

20–25 oysters, shucked and rinsed in cold water

4 stalks bok choy, cut into 2.5-cm (1-in) lengths

4 large eggs

Sweet chilli sauce

Batter

180 g (6^1/$_3$ oz) sweet potato starch

300 ml (10 fl oz / 1^1/$_4$ cups) water

60 g (2^1/$_4$ oz) Chinese chives, finely chopped

Seasoning

^{1}/$_2$ tsp salt

^{1}/$_2$ tsp sugar

^{1}/$_4$ tsp sesame oil

^{1}/$_4$ tsp ground white pepper

1. Mix the ingredients for the batter with the seasoning. The batter should be even without any lumps.

2. Heat 2 Tbsp oil in a large frying pan over medium heat. Add 5–6 oysters and stir-fry for 20 seconds, then push the oysters to the side of the frying pan.

3. Pour a ladleful of batter into the frying pan, keeping it to one side. When the batter turns translucent, arrange the oysters on the batter.

4. Using another pan, heat 2 Tbsp oil over medium heat. Add the bok choy and stir-fry for 20 seconds, then place some of the bok choy over the oysters.

5. Crack an egg into the frying pan, next to the batter. Using a spatula, break up the yolk.

6. Flip the batter onto the egg and fry until the omelette is golden brown on both sides.

7. Transfer to a plate. Repeat to make another 3 omelettes.

8. Serve immediately with sweet chilli sauce.

 Note: The bok choy can be substituted with other green leafy vegetables of choice.

OMELETTE WITH PRESERVED RADISH

菜脯蛋

Serves 4

This simple omelette is very popular in Taiwan where it is enjoyed throughout the day, be it for breakfast, lunch or dinner. That's how much we love this dish! Instead of cooking it into an omelette, the eggs can also be scrambled.

2 Tbsp cooking oil

45 g (1¹/₂ oz) preserved chopped radish

4 large eggs, beaten

A pinch of ground white pepper

1. Heat the oil in a frying pan over high heat. Add the preserved chopped radish and stir-fry for 20 seconds.

2. Lower to medium heat and add the eggs. Leave to cook for about 10 seconds, then use a spatula or fork to gently stir the eggs a little. Let cook until golden brown on the underside.

3. Flip the omelette over to brown the other side.

4. Dish out and serve immediately.

 Note: The salt content varies with the different brands of preserved chopped radish. If the preserved radish is too salty for your liking, remove excess salt by rinsing it with water and leaving it to soak for 10–20 minutes before use. I do not use extra salt when preparing this dish as I find the preserved chopped radish is sufficiently salty.

SOY SAUCE EGGS 滷蛋

Makes 6

Soy sauce eggs are also known as *lu dan* or stewed eggs, and they are a very common dish in Taiwan. When I was living in Taiwan, I would always add a soy sauce egg with my lunch box or have it with my minced pork rice or noodles. Soy sauce eggs are left to sit in the mixture of soy sauce and spices overnight so the eggs will take on the flavour of the sauce, so you can imagine, these eggs are really tasty.

6 large eggs, at room temperature

Sauce

1 litre (32 fl oz / 4 cups) water

100 ml (3^1/$_2$ fl oz) light soy sauce

1 Tbsp dark soy sauce

1 tsp sugar

2 slices ginger

2 spring onions, sliced

1 red chilli

2 cardamom pods

^{1}/$_2$ cinnamon stick or a pinch of ground cinnamon

^{1}/$_4$ tsp cumin

1 star anise

1. This dish must be prepared a day in advance.

2. Place all the ingredients for the sauce in a saucepan or stockpot. Bring to a boil, then simmer over low heat for 1 hour. Set aside to cool.

3. Place the eggs in a pot of water and bring to a boil, stirring constantly. When the water starts to boil, reduce to low heat and simmer for 4^1/$_2$ minutes.

4. Remove the eggs and place immediately into a basin of cold water to cool. Peel the eggs when they are cool enough to handle.

5. Place the peeled eggs in the cooled sauce. The sauce should cover the eggs completely. Refrigerate for at least 12 hours before serving.

 Note: Using eggs at room temperature and bringing them to boil together with the water ensures that the shells will not crack due to a sudden change in temperature. Stirring the eggs while the water boils will also ensure that the yolks will set in the centre of the whites.

STEAMED EGG WITH SEAFOOD SAUCE

海鮮蒸蛋

Serves 2

This quick and easy dish is commonly prepared in Taiwanese households. The flavour of this dish is very light and you can taste the freshness of the seafood. Serve it with other side dishes and rice for a complete meal or simply with rice for a light meal.

2 dried shiitake mushrooms, soaked in hot water to soften

6 prawns, peeled and deveined

80 g (2⁴/₅ oz) squid, cleaned (page 82) and cut into rings, or use other seafood of choice such as scallops, mussels or fish

1 tsp cooking oil

1 Tbsp edamame beans

Marinade

¹/₄ tsp salt

A pinch of ground white pepper

¹/₂ tsp potato starch or cornflour

¹/₄ tsp rice wine

Steamed Egg

375 ml (12 fl oz / 1¹/₂ cups) water

1 tsp salt

¹/₂ tsp bonito powder (optional)

4 large eggs, beaten

Sauce

¹/₂ tsp oyster sauce

¹/₄ tsp sesame oil

¹/₂ tsp light soy sauce

¹/₄ tsp potato starch or cornflour, mixed with 180 ml (6 fl oz / ³/₄ cup) water

1. Squeeze any excess water from the mushrooms and slice finely. Set aside.

2. Mix the prawns with the marinade and set aside for 5–10 minutes.

3. Prepare the steamed egg. Heat the water, salt and bonito powder, if using, in a pot until hot but not boiling. Add to the beaten eggs while stirring all the time.

4. Strain the egg mixture through a sieve into a heatproof bowl or deep plate. Add half the seafood to the egg mixture. Cover with plastic wrap and steam for about 15 minutes.

5. Heat the oil in a pan over medium heat. Add the shiitake mushrooms, remaining seafood and ingredients for the sauce. Bring to a boil and pour over the steamed egg.

6. Garnish with edamame beans or as desired and serve.

FISH AND SEAFOOD

SQUID WITH TAIWANESE FIVE-FLAVOUR SAUCE 五味花枝

Serves 4

Taiwanese five-flavour sauce is so-called because it is a mix of sweet, sour, salty, spicy and bitter flavours. It is the perfect condiment to go with fresh seafood and it is a must-have table condiment for the Taiwanese. There are many variations of five-flavour sauce and everyone has their favourite. Feel free to vary the amount of ingredients added to the sauce according to taste.

500 g (1 lb 1¹/₂ oz) squid

Water, as needed

2.5-cm (1-in) knob ginger, sliced

Taiwanese Five-flavour Sauce

1 Tbsp finely chopped garlic

1 tsp finely chopped ginger

1 tsp finely chopped red chilli

1 tsp finely chopped spring onion

Seasoning

1 Tbsp sugar

2 Tbsp ketchup

1 Tbsp thick soy sauce

1 tsp light soy sauce

¹/₄ tsp black vinegar

¹/₄ tsp rice vinegar

A pinch of ground white pepper

1. Place the ingredients for the five-flavour sauce and seasoning in a bowl and mix evenly. Set aside for at least 30 minutes.

2. Clean the squid. Holding the head with one hand and the body with the other hand, separate the head from the body. The entrails should follow. Cut the tentacles from the head and discard the head. Push out and discard the beak from the top of the tentacles. Rinse and set the tentacles aside. Pull the purple skin from the squid tube and discard. Remove and discard the translucent quill from the tube. Slit the tube in half and remove any remaining entrails. Rinse well.

3. Place the squid tube flat on a cutting board, with the inside facing up.

4. Score the squid tube with a criss-cross pattern. Cut into rectangular pieces.

5. Boil a pot of water with ginger in a saucepan and blanch the squid briefly (about 20 seconds) or until it curls and turns opaque. Remove and plunge immediately into iced water to cool. When the squid is cool, drain well.

6. Serve the squid with the five-flavour sauce on the side.

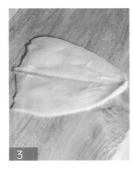

STIR-FRIED SQUID WITH CELERY

芹菜炒花枝

Serves 4

Chinese celery is crunchy and aromatic with a lightness and natural sweetness to it. Combined with lightly cooked squid, this dish is a favourite with many Taiwanese.

130 g (4²/₃ oz) Chinese celery

450 g (1 lb) squid

Water, as needed

1 Tbsp cooking oil

15 g (¹/₂ oz) ginger, peeled and cut into fine strips

15 g (¹/₂ oz) garlic, peeled and finely chopped

15 g (¹/₂ oz) red chilli, cut into strips

Seasoning

¹/₂ tsp salt

¹/₄ tsp sesame oil

1 Tbsp rice wine

1. Rinse the Chinese celery. Pluck and discard the leaves. Slice the celery stalks into 5-cm (2-in) lengths. Set aside.

2. Clean, score and cut the squid. (See page 82 for instructions.)

3. Boil some water in a saucepan and blanch the squid briefly. Remove and plunge immediately into iced water to cool. When the squid is cool, drain well.

4. Heat the oil in a wok over high heat. Add the ginger, garlic and chilli and stir-fry for 20 seconds.

5. Add the celery and stir-fry for 2 minutes.

6. Add the squid and seasoning. Cook for another 3–4 minutes.

7. Dish out and serve immediately.

 Note: You can use Western celery in place of Chinese celery, but the dish will not be as fragrant.

STIR-FRIED OYSTERS AND TOFU WITH BLACK BEAN SAUCE 蔭鼓蚵仔豆腐

Serves 4

This Fujian-style dish is a Taiwanese classic. It is very simple to prepare and it is a perfect example of Taiwanese cooking where the emphasis is placed on using fresh ingredients and keeping true to the original flavour of the ingredients. The black bean sauce gives this dish a real kick, but you need to be careful not to overdo it or it will overpower the dish. In Taiwan, oysters are known as the "milk of the sea" because they are fat and juicy in texture, and are rich in vitamins and minerals.

20 oysters, shucked and rinsed in cold water

1 Tbsp potato starch or cornflour

150 g (5^1/$_3$ oz) silken tofu, cut into 2.5-cm (1-in) cubes

2 Tbsp cooking oil

30 g (1 oz) black beans, soaked in 1 Tbsp rice wine for at least 15 minutes

1 tsp finely chopped ginger

2 tsp finely chopped garlic

1^1/$_2$ tsp chopped spring onion

1 red chilli, cut into strips

Seasoning

2 Tbsp thick soy sauce

1 Tbsp rice wine

1 Tbsp potato starch or cornflour, mixed with 1^1/$_2$ Tbsp water

1. Mix the oysters with the potato starch or cornflour. This will help keep the oysters moist as they cook.

2. Boil some water in a saucepan and blanch the tofu cubes briefly. Drain and set aside.

3. Heat the oil in a wok over medium heat. Drain the black beans and add to the wok. Stir-fry for 10 seconds.

4. Increase to high heat and add the ginger, garlic and spring onion. Stir-fry for 20 seconds.

5. Add the oysters and stir-fry for another 20 seconds.

6. Add the tofu and the seasoning. Cook for 3–5 minutes.

7. Add the chilli and stir-fry for 1 minute.

8. Dish out and serve immediately.

STEAMED PRAWNS WITH GLASS NOODLES AND GARLIC SAUCE

蒜蓉冬粉蒸蝦

Serves 4

Prawn dishes are often served at banquets and receptions in Taiwan because of the bright orange-red colour of the prawns after cooking. In Taiwanese tradition, red is symbolic of good fortune and luck, and hence the brightly coloured prawns make a fitting dish for such happy occasions. For this dish, I added vermicelli while steaming the prawns, so it will absorb all the juices and flavours from the steamed prawns.

12 prawns, rinsed in cold water

100 g (3¹/₂ oz) glass noodles

Garlic Sauce

40 g (1¹/₃ oz) garlic, peeled and finely chopped

30 g (1 oz) spring onion, finely chopped

15 g (¹/₂ oz) red chilli, finely chopped

2 Tbsp thick soy sauce

2 Tbsp light soy sauce

2 Tbsp rice wine

3 Tbsp water

1 tsp sugar

1. Without peeling the prawns, make a slit down the back of the prawns. Remove the black vein. Rinse and set aside.

2. Boil some water in a saucepan and blanch the glass noodles until soft but not cooked through. Remove and plunge into iced water to cool.

3. Place the ingredients for the garlic sauce in a bowl and mix evenly.

4. Place the glass noodles on a shallow steaming plate and arrange the prawns on top. Pour the garlic sauce over the prawns and steam for about 15 minutes until the prawns turn red and are cooked.

5. Serve immediately.

DEEP-FRIED PRAWN ROLLS 炸蝦捲

Makes 24 rolls

This simple snack is quick and easy to do, and it originates from the Tamshui District in Northern Taiwan. Tamshui is an idyllic coastal town known for its street snacks and seafood. These deep-fried rolls are now popular throughout Taiwan and you will find them at many night market stalls.

100 g (3¹/₂ oz) fatty pork loin, cut into small cubes

24 prawns

1 egg white

2 slices ginger, finely chopped

1 tsp finely chopped spring onion

1 Tbsp potato starch or cornflour

24 spring roll sheets

1 egg, beaten

750 ml (24 fl oz / 3 cups) cooking oil

Seasoning

1 tsp salt

¹/₄ tsp ground black pepper

1 Tbsp sesame oil

¹/₂ tsp castor sugar

1. Freeze the pork until it is hard on the outside but soft enough to cut through with a knife. Cut into small cubes.

2. Peel 12 prawns and devein them. Rinse well.

3. Using a food processor, blend the pork with the peeled prawns until the mixture is fine and sticky. Set aside.

4. Boil a pot of water and blanch the remaining prawns until they change colour and are cooked. Peel the prawns and chop roughly.

5. Add the cooked prawns to the pork mixture together with the egg white, ginger, spring onion and potato starch or cornflour. Mix well.

6. Add the seasoning and mix evenly.

7. Spoon ¹/₂ Tbsp prawn filling onto each spring roll sheet. Brush the edges with beaten egg.

8. Fold two opposite corners of the spring roll sheet over to enclose the filling. Twist the two ends to seal the roll.

9. Heat the oil in a wok over medium heat to about 160°C (325°F). Deep-fry the prawn rolls in batches until crisp and golden brown. Drain well.

10. Serve with sweet chilli sauce.

7

8a

8b

STIR-FRIED MUSSELS WITH BASIL
塔香九孔

Serves 4

This popular dish is often found on the menus of seafood restaurants in Taiwan. Basil is commonly used in Taiwanese stir-fries and its amazing fragrance goes well with shellfish.

1 kg (2 lb 3 oz) mussels

Cooking oil, as needed

2 spring onions, finely chopped

1 red chilli, sliced

30 g (1 oz) ginger, peeled and finely chopped

40 g (1¹/₃ oz) garlic, peeled and finely chopped

60 g (2¹/₄ oz) basil

Seasoning

4 Tbsp thick soy sauce

2 Tbsp rice wine

1 tsp sugar

¹/₄ tsp sesame oil

1. Soak the mussels in a basin of cold water for at least 20 minutes for them to expel any sand or grit. Remove the mussels from the water, being careful not to stir up the sand or grit. Scrub the mussels and remove the beards. Rinse well. Drain and set aside.

2. Heat 2 Tbsp oil in a wok over medium heat. Add the spring onions, chilli, ginger and garlic and stir-fry for 5–10 seconds until fragrant.

3. Add the mussels and stir-fry for 1 minute. Cover with a lid and leave to cook for 30 seconds.

4. Add the seasoning and cook over high heat until the liquid has reduced.

5. Add the basil and stir-fry for 10 seconds.

6. Dish out and serve immediately.

STEAMED HALIBUT WITH PICKLED CORDIA 破布子蒸魚

Serves 4

Steamed fish with pickled cordia is a very common dish in Taiwan and it is on the menu of practically every seafood restaurant. Be careful however when you prepare this dish at home, as the pickled cordia has a strong flavour and adding too much can spoil the taste of the dish.

4 slices halibut fillet, each 180–200 g (6^1/$_3$–7 oz)

^{1}/$_2$ tsp salt

2 Tbsp pickled cordia with some pickling liquid

1 tsp finely chopped garlic

1 tsp finely sliced red chilli

30 g (1 oz) spring onion, finely sliced

Seasoning

1 tsp sugar

^{1}/$_2$ tsp salt

A pinch of ground white pepper

1 Tbsp rice wine

^{1}/$_4$ tsp sesame oil

1 Tbsp light soy sauce

1. Rinse the fish and pat dry with paper towels. Rub the salt over the fish and set aside for 10 minutes.

2. Mix the cordia, garlic and seasoning in a bowl and set aside for 5 minutes.

3. Place the fish on a steaming plate and cover with the cordia and garlic seasoning. Top with the sliced chilli and spring onion.

4. Place the fish in a steamer and steam over medium heat for about 20 minutes or until the fish is cooked through.

5. Serve immediately.

DEEP-FRIED FISH AND PORK ROLLS

炸雞卷

Makes 3–4 rolls

This dish came about in the olden days when people were more careful about not letting food go to waste. If there were any leftovers, it would be wrapped up in dried tofu skin and deep-fried to create a new dish. Today, this dish is specially prepared and can be served as an appetiser, as a side dish with other dishes or as finger food.

200 g (7 oz) pork loin

450 g (1 lb) fish paste (page 62)

50 g (1³/₄ oz) onion, peeled and finely chopped

50 g (1³/₄ oz) carrot, peeled and finely chopped

3–4 sheets dried tofu skin, each about 18 x 18-cm (7 x 7-in)

2 Tbsp plain flour, mixed with 3 Tbsp water

1 litre (32 fl oz / 4 cups) cooking oil

Sweet chilli sauce

Marinade

1 Tbsp thick soy sauce

¹/₂ Tbsp light soy sauce

1 tsp rice wine

¹/₂ Tbsp sugar

¹/₂ tsp Chinese five-spice powder

Seasoning

1 tsp salt

¹/₄ tsp ground white pepper

1 tsp sugar

1. Cut the pork loin into 3–4 long thin strips. Mix well with the marinade and set aside for 30 minutes.

2. Place the fish paste, onion and carrot in a bowl and mix evenly. Add the seasoning and stir until well mixed. Divide the mixture into 3–4 equal portions.

3. Wipe a sheet of dried tofu skin with a clean damp cloth. Spoon a portion of the filling onto it, then place a strip of marinated pork loin in the centre. Press the pork into the fish paste so it is covered by the fish paste. Wrap the tofu skin over the filling and shape it into a cylinder. Seal the edges of the tofu skin with the flour and water mixture. Repeat to make 3–4 rolls.

4. Heat the oil in a wok to 180°C (350°F). Lower 2–3 rolls into the hot oil and turn off the heat. Let the rolls sit in the hot oil for 1 minute. Reheat the oil over low heat and cook for 5–10 minutes until the rolls are golden brown. Remove and drain well. Repeat to cook the other 2 rolls.

5. Slice the rolls and serve with sweet chilli sauce.

 Note: This method of cooking the fish and pork rolls is similar to the method employed for the dragon phoenix legs (page 62). This will ensure that the filling is thoroughly cooked without burning the tofu skin.

SOUPS

GINGER AND SESAME OIL CHICKEN SOUP 麻油雞

Serves 4

This soup is typically enjoyed during the cold winter months as the rice wine helps to warm the body. Sometimes, this dish is also prepared using only rice wine with no added water. In Taiwan, expectant mothers do not consume this soup as it contains a lot of alcohol and dark sesame oil is also thought to cause womb contractions.

2 Tbsp dark sesame oil

10 slices ginger (evenly sliced)

6 chicken thighs, approximately 800 g (1³/₄ lb), cut into bite-size pieces

625 ml (20 fl oz / 2¹/₂ cups) rice wine

625 ml (20 fl oz / 2¹/₂ cups) water

1 tsp salt

1 tsp sugar

1. Heat the dark sesame oil in a wok over low heat. Add the ginger and stir-fry until golden brown and crisp. Do this over low heat so as not to burn the ginger. Burnt ginger will leave a bitter taste.

2. Add the chicken and stir-fry over high heat until the meat turns white.

3. Transfer everything to a stockpot and add the rice wine and water. Bring to a boil, then simmer over low heat for 1 hour.

4. Season with salt and sugar.

5. Dish out and serve immediately.

Note: This dish can be prepared using any part of the chicken. I have used chicken thighs, but you can also use a whole chicken, cut into pieces.

MUSTARD GREEN CHICKEN SOUP

長年菜雞湯

Serves 4

This soup is traditionally served during the Lunar New Year as the long stalks of mustard greens are symbolic of long life. Mustard greens are often used in soups and stir-fries in Taiwanese cooking as it is not just tasty, but also one of the most nutritious green vegetables, full of antioxidants and vitamins.

1 medium-size chicken, cut into pieces

3 slices ginger

1.5 litres (48 fl oz / 6 cups) water, or as needed

800 g (1³/₄ lb) mustard greens

1 tsp salt

¹/₄ tsp ground white pepper

1. Boil a large pot of water and blanch the chicken briefly. Drain and rinse the chicken with cold water. This step will clean and rid the chicken of any unpleasant smells and impurities.

2. Place the chicken into a stockpot and add the ginger. Add the water so the ingredients are completely covered. Add more water if necessary. Bring to a boil, then lower the heat and simmer for about 1¹/₂ hours until the chicken is cooked through and tender.

3. Rinse the mustard greens and drain well. Cut them into short lengths.

4. Add the mustard greens and cook for a few minutes. Season the soup with the salt and pepper.

5. Dish out and serve.

PICKLED PINEAPPLE AND BITTER GOURD CHICKEN SOUP 鳳梨苦瓜雞湯

Serves 4

In Taiwan, free-range chicken is used in this soup for its sweet and firm texture that complements the soft and melting texture of the boiled bitter gourd. You will notice that no other seasoning is used in this dish as the strongly flavoured pineapple bean sauce is sufficient. Taste and adjust the seasoning as necessary.

4 chicken legs, including drumsticks and thighs, cut into big pieces

200 g (7 oz) bitter gourd

2 slices ginger

1.25 litres (40 fl oz / 5 cups) water

100 g (3¹/₂ oz) pineapple bean sauce

1. Boil a large pot of water and blanch the chicken briefly. Drain and rinse the chicken with cold water. This step will clean and rid the chicken of any unpleasant smells and impurities.

2. Cut the bitter gourd in half lengthwise, then use a spoon to scoop out the soft centre. Cut into large cubes.

3. Place the chicken, ginger and water into a stockpot. Bring to a boil, then simmer over low heat for 40 minutes.

4. Add the bitter gourd and simmer for another 20 minutes.

5. Add the pineapple bean sauce and bring it to a boil.

6. Dish out and serve.

Note: Pineapple bean sauce is sometimes also known as Taiwanese pickled pineapple. It is available in jars from Chinese supermarkets or stores specialising in Taiwanese food products. Unfortunately, there is no substitute for this ingredient.

PORK BALL SOUP 貢丸湯

Serves 4

The story behind this dish is of a filial son. Towards the end of the Ming Dynasty, there lived a man and his mother in a small seaside town in Fuzhou. His father had passed away and his mother had gone blind from crying so much after her husband died. The family was poor and the man studied and worked hard, finally landing a job in the city. One of his goals was to buy pork for his mother to enjoy. But by the time he saved enough money, his mother was old and could no longer chew pork. The man thought hard about how he could overcome this, and he began working the pork until it was really soft, finally coming up with this pork ball soup for his mother.

Pork Balls

600 g (1 lb 5^1/$_3$ oz) lean pork

100 g (3^1/$_2$ oz) fatty pork

2 tsp salt

1 Tbsp sugar

^{1}/$_4$ tsp ground white pepper

1 tsp baking powder

1.25 litres (40 fl oz / 5 cups) water

2 tsp chopped spring onion or Chinese celery

Seasoning

^{1}/$_2$ tsp salt, or to taste

^{1}/$_4$ tsp ground white pepper

1 tsp crisp-fried shallots

1. Prepare the pork balls. Freeze both the lean and fatty pork until they are hard on the outside but soft enough to cut through with a knife. Cut into small cubes.

2. Using a food processor, blend the lean and fatty pork until the mixture is fine and sticky. Transfer to a large mixing bowl. Add the salt, sugar, pepper and baking powder and mix well.

3. Using clean hands, gather the mixture and throw it back into the bowl. Do this 20–30 times. Set aside.

4. Bring the water to a boil in a pot. Turn off the heat. Form small balls from the pork mixture and add to the pot of hot water.

5. Reheat the water over low heat and cook the pork balls until they float. Remove the cooked pork balls with a slotted spoon and set aside.

6. Return the water to the boil. Season with the salt, pepper and crisp-fried onions. Add the pork balls and cook for 2–3 minutes.

7. Ladle the pork balls and soup into serving bowls. Garnish with spring onion or Chinese celery. Serve immediately.

WHITE RADISH AND PORK RIB SOUP

白蘿蔔排骨湯

Serves 4

This is a very common soup prepared in Taiwanese households as it is thought that the boiled pork ribs will provide children with much-needed calcium. The white radish gives this dish a natural sweetness and is refreshing to eat.

320 g (11$\frac{1}{4}$ oz) pork ribs, cut into short lengths

1 litre (32 fl oz / 4 cups) water

1 Tbsp rice wine

2 slices ginger

200 g (7 oz) white radish, peeled and cut into 2.5-cm (1-in) cubes

Salt, to taste

Ground white pepper, to taste

1. Boil a pot of water and blanch the ribs briefly to remove any impurities. Drain and rinse with cold water.

2. Place the ribs, water, rice wine and ginger into a stockpot. Bring to a boil, then simmer over low heat for 1 hour.

3. Add the white radish and cook for about 30 minutes until the meat on the ribs are soft and tender.

4. Season with salt and pepper to taste.

5. Dish out. Garnish as desired and serve.

WHITE RADISH AND FRIED PORK RIB SOUP 排骨酥湯

Serves 4

This is a very popular street food in Taiwan. Just as with the white radish and pork rib soup (page 108), this dish has a natural sweetness from the white radish and is extra tasty given the fried pork ribs. Use meaty pork ribs to make this dish more enjoyable.

400 g (14¹/₃ oz) pork ribs, cut into short lengths

Sweet potato starch, as needed

1 litre (32 fl oz / 4 cups) cooking oil

30 g (1 oz) spring onion, cut into 3-cm (1¹/₄-in) lengths

15 g (¹/₂ oz) garlic, peeled and finely chopped

1.25 litres (40 fl oz / 5 cups) water

300 g (11 oz) white radish, peeled and cut into 2.5-cm (1-in) cubes

¹/₂ tsp salt, or to taste

¹/₄ tsp ground white pepper, or to taste

Marinade

1 tsp finely chopped garlic

1 Tbsp light soy sauce

1 Tbsp rice wine

¹/₄ tsp salt

1 tsp sugar

¹/₄ tsp ground white pepper

¹/₄ tsp Chinese five-spice powder

1. Place the ribs and marinade in a bowl. Mix well. Cover and set aside in the refrigerator for at least 1 hour.

2. Coat the marinated ribs with some sweet potato starch and set aside for 10 minutes.

3. Heat the oil in a wok over medium heat. Add the ribs and deep-fry until golden brown and cooked through. Drain and set aside.

4. Leave 2 Tbsp oil in the wok and reheat. Add the spring onion and garlic and stir-fry until the garlic is just golden brown.

5. Add the water and bring to a boil, then simmer over low heat for 30 minutes. Strain the soup.

6. Divide the fried pork ribs, white radish and stock among 4 heatproof serving bowls. Place the bowls into a steamer or rice cooker and steam for 45 minutes to 1 hour until the radish is cooked and tender.

7. Season the soup with salt and pepper. Garnish as desired and serve.

PORK AND FISH DUMPLING SOUP 肉羹湯

Serves 4

This is a very popular soup in Taiwan. Potato starch or cornflour is added to give it a thick and sticky consistency. Those not accustomed to such dishes may not take to it at first, but it is a dish that really grows on you. There are many variations to this dish and most Taiwanese chefs will have their own recipes for this soup.

Dumplings

350 g (12 oz) fatty pork

30 g (1 oz) ice cubes

$^1/_2$ tsp salt

1 tsp sugar

1 tsp potato starch or cornflour

1 tsp crisp-fried shallots

$^1/_4$ tsp Chinese five-spice powder

$^1/_2$ tsp ground white pepper

$^1/_4$ tsp sesame oil

150 g (5$^1/_3$ oz) fish paste (page 62)

Soup

2 Tbsp cooking oil

15 g ($^1/_2$ oz) garlic, peeled and finely chopped

1.25 litres (40 fl oz / 5 cups) stock or water from cooking dumplings

40 g (1$^1/_3$ oz) bonito flakes

40 g (1$^1/_3$ oz) black fungus, soaked to soften, then cut into strips

60 g (2$^1/_4$ oz) carrot, peeled and cut into strips

40 g (1$^1/_3$ oz) bamboo shoot, cut into strips

$^1/_2$ tsp salt

1 tsp light soy sauce

10 g ($^1/_3$ oz) rock sugar

1 tsp black vinegar

$^1/_4$ tsp ground white pepper

$^1/_4$ tsp sesame oil

1 Tbsp potato starch or cornflour, mixed with 1 Tbsp water

1. Prepare the dumplings. Freeze the pork until it is hard on the outside but soft enough to cut through with a knife. Cut into small cubes.

2. Using a food processor, blend the pork until the mixture is fine and sticky. Add the ice cubes, salt, sugar, potato starch or cornflour, crisp-fried shallots, five-spice powder, pepper and sesame oil and blend for 10 minutes. Transfer the pork paste to a bowl, cover and refrigerate for 30 minutes.

3. Add the fish paste to the pork paste and mix evenly.

4. Boil some water in a saucepan.

5. Shape 2 tablespoonfuls of the pork and fish paste into a ball and add to the boiling water to cook. Repeat with the rest of the paste. When the dumplings float, they are done. Remove with a slotted spoon and set aside.

6. Prepare the soup. Heat the oil in a wok over medium heat. Add the garlic and stir-fry for 10 seconds. Add the stock or the water from cooking the dumplings and the bonito flakes. Bring to a boil, then simmer over low heat for 15 minutes.

7. Strain the stock into a pot and bring to a boil. Add the black fungus, carrot and bamboo shoot and return to the boil.

8. Add the dumplings, salt, soy sauce, rock sugar, black vinegar, pepper and sesame oil. Let the soup return to the boil.

9. Stir in the potato starch or cornflour slurry and allow the soup to boil once again.

10. Ladle into serving bowls. Garnish as desired and serve.

SALMON TOFU MISO SOUP 鮭魚味噌湯

Serves 3

Modern Taiwanese cuisine is largely influenced by Japanese and Chinese cuisine, and one such dish is salmon tofu miso soup. The salmon can be replaced with any kind of fish you like, but in Taiwan, salmon is the preferred choice. Serve this with other side dishes and rice for a wholesome and satisfying meal.

300 g (11 oz) salmon fillet, skinned

350 g (12 oz) silken tofu

800 ml (26 fl oz) water

2 Tbsp bonito flakes or 1 Tbsp bonito powder

1 tsp finely chopped ginger

1 tsp white miso paste

1 tsp rice wine

1. Cut the salmon and tofu into 2.5-cm (1-in) cubes.

2. Place the water, bonito flakes or powder and ginger into a saucepan. Bring to a boil and simmer for 30 minutes.

3. Strain the soup back into the pan and bring to a boil. Turn to low heat and add the salmon and tofu. Simmer for 15 minutes.

4. Mix the miso paste with the rice wine and add to the soup. Stir gently to avoid breaking up the salmon and tofu. Simmer for another 10 minutes.

5. Dish out. Garnish as desired and serve.

VEGETABLES AND TOFU

STIR-FRIED AUBERGINE WITH BASIL

客家炒茄子

Serves 3

I'm not a big fan of aubergine, but I really like this dish. My mother cooked this often when I was young and I find the combination of aubergine and basil delicious. Aubergine tends to have an aftertaste, but basil, especially Thai basil, helps to rid the aubergine of this.

350 g (12 oz) aubergines (eggplant/brinjal)

30 g (1 oz) Thai basil

450 ml (15 fl oz / 1⁴/₅ cups) + 1 Tbsp cooking oil

15 g (¹/₂ oz) garlic, peeled and roughly chopped

15 g (¹/₂ oz) red chilli, sliced

¹/₂ tsp sugar

2 Tbsp light soy sauce

1. Trim the tops off the aubergines. Cut into quarters lengthways, then into short lengths about 4 cm (1¹/₂ in) long.

2. Rinse the basil and pluck the leaves. Discard the stems.

3. Heat 450 ml (15 fl oz) oil to 150°C (300°F) in a wok and deep-fry the aubergines for about 10 seconds. Drain and set aside.

4. In a clean wok, heat 1 Tbsp oil over high heat. Add the garlic and chilli and stir-fry until aromatic.

5. Add the deep-fried aubergines, sugar and soy sauce and stir-fry for 2–3 minutes.

6. Add the basil leaves and cover the wok with a lid. Turn off the heat and leave for 1 minute. Dish out and serve.

Note: Thai basil works best for this dish due to its strong taste. If using other types of basil, you will need more than 30 g (1 oz) of the leaves.

STIR-FRIED PICKLED BAMBOO SHOOT WITH SPICY MINCED BEEF 醃筍炒牛肉末

Serves 4

Traditionally, food was preserved by drying or pickling so that they could be stored for future consumption, and this dish features one such ingredient, pickled bamboo shoot. This is one of my favourite dishes that my grandma cooks. Whenever I visit Taiwan, I never fail to ask her to cook this dish for me and she is always happy to oblige. This dish is perfect eaten with white rice.

400 g (14^1/$_3$ oz) minced beef

2 Tbsp cooking oil

15 g (^{1}/$_2$ oz) garlic, peeled and chopped

15 g (^{1}/$_2$ oz) red chilli, sliced

400 g (14^1/$_3$ oz) pickled bamboo shoot, cut into cubes

Marinade

1^1/$_2$ tsp sugar

2 Tbsp light soy sauce

1 tsp potato starch or cornflour

^{1}/$_2$ tsp rice wine

Seasoning

^{1}/$_2$ tsp salt

1 tsp dark soy sauce

1 Tbsp light soy sauce

1. Place the minced beef and marinade in a bowl and mix well. Set aside for at least 30 minutes.

2. Heat the oil in a wok over high heat. Add the garlic and chilli and stir-fry until aromatic.

3. Add the pickled bamboo shoots and stir-fry for 2 minutes.

4. Add the minced beef and seasoning and stir-fry until the meat is cooked.

5. Dish out and serve immediately.

THREE-CUP MUSHROOMS 三杯菇

Serves 4

The Taiwanese are fond of preparing dishes using three principle ingredients in equal proportions, namely sesame oil, soy sauce and rice wine, hence the name "three-cup". There are many three-cup dishes in Taiwanese cuisine, and they include three-cup chicken, three-cup duck, three-cup thousand-year-old egg, three-cup squid and three-cup fish. For this dish, you can add any type of fresh mushrooms available.

30 g (1 oz) basil

Dark sesame oil for stir-frying

4 thin slices ginger

10 cloves garlic, peeled and left whole

15 g (1/2 oz) red chilli, sliced

500 g (1 lb 1 1/2 oz) fresh mushrooms of choice, wiped and trimmed

Seasoning

2 Tbsp dark sesame oil

1 tsp sugar

1 Tbsp thick soy sauce

2 Tbsp light soy sauce

1. Rinse the basil and pluck the leaves. Discard the stems.

2. Heat some dark sesame oil in a wok over medium heat. Add the ginger and stir-fry until the ginger turns golden brown and crisp.

3. Add the garlic and chilli and stir-fry for 30 seconds.

4. Increase to high heat and add the mushrooms, followed by the seasoning. Stir-fry until the sauce is reduced.

5. Add the basil leaves and stir-fry for 10 seconds.

6. Dish out and serve immediately.

SALTED MUSTARD GREENS WITH TOFU AND EDAMAME BEANS

雪裡紅毛豆炒豆干

Serves 4

Salted mustard greens are used in many Taiwanese dishes. Here, it is cooked with tofu and edamame beans. Although salted mustard greens must be prepared in advance, it is not difficult to do. Carrot leaves and rapeseed (*yu choy*) can also be used in place of mustard greens.

2 Tbsp cooking oil

1/4 tsp finely chopped garlic

1 red chilli, sliced

100 g (3¹/₂ oz) edamame beans, blanched

200 g (7 oz) extra firm tofu, cut into 1-cm (¹/₂-in) cubes

Seasoning

100 ml (3¹/₂ fl oz) water

1 Tbsp light soy sauce

1 tsp salt

¹/₂ tsp sesame oil

Salted Mustard Greens

500 g (1 lb 1¹/₂ oz) mustard greens

30 g (1 oz) sea salt

1. Prepare the salted mustard greens 3 days in advance. Rinse and drain the mustard greens. Sprinkle the sea salt over the mustard greens and rub the salt in gently. Leave for 1 hour.

2. Squeeze to remove the water from the mustard greens. Place in a container with a lid and set aside in a cool, dark place for 3 days before using. After this, the salted mustard greens can be kept refrigerated for up to 7 days.

3. Rinse the salted mustard greens and squeeze dry. Chop finely and set aside.

4. Heat the oil in a wok over medium heat. Add the garlic and chilli and stir-fry for about 10 seconds.

5. Add the salted mustard greens and stir-fry for 1 minute.

6. Add the edamame beans, tofu and seasoning. Stir-fry until the ingredients are almost dry.

7. Dish out and serve immediately.

TAIWANESE-STYLE KIMCHI 台式泡菜

Serves 4

Taiwanese-style kimchi is different from Korean kimchi in that it tastes sweet and sour but it is not spicy at all. This recipe provides a quick way of making Taiwanese-style kimchi and this is how I do it whenever I want to have some Taiwanese-style kimchi. This is the perfect accompaniment to stinky tofu, another Taiwanese favourite.

300 g (11 oz) white cabbage, torn into smaller pieces

150 g (5^1/$_3$ oz) cucumber, sliced

80 g (2^4/$_5$ oz) carrot, peeled and cut into strips

2 thin slices ginger

1 red chilli, sliced

^{1}/$_4$ tsp ground Sichuan pepper or 1 tsp Sichuan peppercorns

1^1/$_2$ Tbsp salt

2^1/$_2$ Tbsp sugar, or to taste

3^1/$_2$ Tbsp rice vinegar, or to taste

200 ml (7 fl oz) water

1. Place the cabbage, cucumber, carrot, ginger and chilli into a clean plastic bag with the Sichuan pepper and salt. Seal and gently shake the bag for 30 seconds, making sure the ingredients are evenly mixed. Set aside for 1–2 minutes.

2. Open the bag and add the sugar and vinegar. Seal and gently shake the bag for another 30 seconds.

3. Add the water and leave to marinate for 1^1/$_2$ hours before serving.

4. The kimchi can be stored in a clean, airtight jar and kept refrigerated for up to 7 days.

BRAISED CHINESE CABBAGE 滷白菜

Serves 4

The simplicity of this typical Taiwanese home-style dish belies its flavour. The longer the Chinese cabbage is left to stew, the better it tastes. The flavour of this dish improves with keeping, so prepare a larger portion to ensure you have leftovers for the next day.

700 g (1¹/₂ lb) Chinese cabbage, cut into big pieces

4 dried shiitake mushrooms, soaked in hot water to soften

30 g (1 oz) dried prawns, soaked in hot water to soften

1 Tbsp cooking oil

15 g (¹/₂ oz) garlic, peeled and finely chopped

15 g (¹/₂ oz) spring onion, cut into 3-cm (1¹/₄-in) lengths

300 ml (10 fl oz / 1¹/₄ cups) water

Seasoning

¹/₂ tsp salt

¹/₂ tsp sugar

¹/₄ tsp ground white pepper

1 tsp bonito powder (optional)

1 Tbsp rice wine

1. Boil a pot of water and blanch the Chinese cabbage briefly. Drain and set aside.

2. Squeeze the excess water from the shiitake mushrooms and reserve the soaking liquid. Slice the mushrooms thinly and set aside.

3. Drain the prawns and set aside.

4. Heat the oil in a saucepan over medium heat. Add the garlic and spring onion and stir-fry until fragrant.

5. Add the mushrooms and dried prawns and stir-fry for 2 minutes.

6. Add the cabbage, water and seasoning. Bring to a boil, then simmer over low heat for 30 minutes until the cabbage is tender.

7. Dish out. Garnish as desired and serve.

BAMBOO SHOOT SALAD 涼筍沙拉

Serves 3

There are several different types of bamboo shoot available in Taiwan, and they are all delicious, hence you will find many dishes that feature bamboo shoot in Taiwanese cooking. This is one of my favourite dishes featuring bamboo shoot, and it is the first dish that I always ask my grandmother to cook for me whenever I go back to visit Taiwan. Being a salad, it is light and helps cool the body in the summer.

2 kg (4 lb 6 oz) fresh bamboo shoot, with skin

1 tsp salt

Water, as needed

Taiwanese-style mayonnaise, to taste (page 36)

1. Do not peel the bamboo shoot. Place it into a stockpot with the salt and add enough water to cover the bamboo shoot completely.

2. Cover the pot and bring the water to a boil. Lower the heat and simmer for 1 hour.

3. Turn off the heat and leave the bamboo shoot to cool in the pot. When cool, remove the bamboo shoot and refrigerate to chill.

4. Peel the bamboo shoot and cut into 2.5-cm (1-in) pieces. Arrange on a serving plate and drizzle with Taiwanese-style mayonnaise. Garnish as desired and serve.

HAKKA-STYLE STUFFED TOFU

客家鑲豆腐

Serves 4

This is a must-have dish for Hakka banquets in Taiwan, and this is the story of how it became a mainstay of Hakka cuisine. The founding emperor of the Ming Dynasty, the Hongwu Emperor, Zhu Yuanzhang, was born into a poor family and became orphaned at a young age. He worked in a restaurant to eke out a living and this dish was very popular there. After becoming emperor, he often ordered his chefs to cook this dish for him, making it a mainstay in the palace menu.

2 dried shiitake mushrooms, soaked in hot water to soften

200 g (7 oz) minced pork

30 g (1 oz) spring onions, finely chopped

600 g (1 lb 5$\frac{1}{3}$ oz) firm tofu

Seasoning

2 Tbsp light soy sauce

$\frac{1}{4}$ tsp sesame oil

1 tsp sugar

$\frac{1}{4}$ tsp salt

Ground white pepper, to taste

Sauce

90 ml (3 fl oz / $\frac{3}{8}$ cup) stock (page 153)

1 Tbsp thick soy sauce

$\frac{1}{4}$ tsp dark soy sauce

$\frac{1}{2}$ tsp sugar

1. Squeeze any excess water from the mushrooms and chop finely. Mix with the minced pork, spring onions and seasoning. Set aside to marinate for 15–20 minutes.

2. Slice the tofu into squares, each about 1.5-cm (¾-in) thick.

3. Using a teaspoon, make a well in the middle of each tofu square and fill with the mushroom and pork mixture.

4. Place the stuffed tofu on a steaming plate and steam for 20–30 minutes over high heat.

5. Place the ingredients for the sauce into a small saucepan. Bring to a boil, then simmer over low heat for 20 minutes, or until the sauce is reduced.

6. Pour the sauce over the steamed stuffed tofu. Garnish as desired and serve immediately.

STEAMED TOFU WITH PRAWNS 芙蓉豆腐

Serves 4

Tofu is a very common ingredient in Chinese and Taiwanese cooking and it is prepared in many different ways including stir-frying, pan-frying, steaming, stewing and deep-frying. In this typical home-style dish, it is steamed with prawn paste. Tofu is not just tasty, but also high in protein, vitamins, calcium and minerals and low in calories, sodium and fat.

500 g (1 lb 1^1/$_2$ oz) firm tofu

Salt, as needed

120 g (4^1/$_3$ oz) prawns

^{1}/$_2$ tsp finely chopped ginger

Seasoning

^{1}/$_4$ tsp salt

^{1}/$_4$ tsp rice wine

1 tsp light soy sauce

^{1}/$_4$ tsp ground white pepper

Sauce

150 ml (5 fl oz) stock (page 153)

1 Tbsp oyster sauce

1 tsp sugar

1 tsp potato starch or cornflour

1. Remove the tofu from its packaging. Drain well and pat dry. Sprinkle some salt on the tofu and leave for a few minutes.

2. Slice the tofu into 2.5-cm (1-in) slabs, then use a cookie cutter to cut the tofu into attractive shapes.

3. Using a teaspoon, dig a small hole in the middle of each piece of tofu. Place on a steaming plate and set aside.

4. Peel and devein the prawns. Rinse and chop roughly, then place in a food processor with the seasoning. Process into a paste. Transfer to a bowl.

5. Roll the prawn paste into small balls and place a ball into each hollowed-out tofu piece.

6. Place the tofu in a steamer over medium heat. Steam for 10–15 minutes until the prawn paste is cooked through. Remove from the steamer.

7. Place the ingredients for the sauce in a small saucepan and bring to a boil, stirring occasionally until the sauce is slightly thickened.

8. Drizzle the sauce over the tofu. Garnish as desired and serve.

SNACKS AND DESSERTS

TARO AND SWEET POTATO BALLS

芋圓和地瓜圓

Serves 8–10

This is a traditional dessert from a town called Jiufen in Northern Taiwan. These balls are said to have been created by a woman named Tsai. Madam Tsai was from Yilan County and she moved to the bustling mining town of Ruifang after marriage. There, Madam Tsai began a business making treats for children using ingredients that were readily available. After several tries, she came up with this recipe. It was an instant hit with everyone who tried them and this dessert has since become an immensely popular dessert associated with both Jiufen and Ruifang.

Syrup

900 ml (30 fl oz) water

10 g (1/3 oz) ginger

500 g (1 lb 1 1/2 oz) dark brown sugar

Taro Balls

400 g (14 1/3 oz) taro, peeled and cut into cubes

50 g (1 3/4 oz) sugar

150 g (5 1/3 oz) tapioca flour

50 ml (1 2/3 fl oz) water

Sweet Potato Balls

400 g (14 1/3 oz) sweet potatoes, peeled and cut into cubes

50 g (1 3/4 oz) sugar

150 g (5 1/3 oz) tapioca flour

50 ml (1 2/3 fl oz) water

1. Place the ingredients for the syrup into a stockpot. Bring to a boil, then simmer over low heat until the liquid is reduced by half. Set aside to cool.

2. Prepare the taro balls and sweet potato balls separately, but using the same method. Steam the taro/sweet potatoes until tender, then mash and mix with the sugar while hot. Add the tapioca flour and water and knead until the mixture comes together. If the mixture is sticky, add a little more tapioca flour and knead again until it is not sticky. Roll the mixture into a long roll and cut into 2.5-cm (1-in) lengths.

3. Boil a pot of water and gently lower the taro and sweet potato balls into the boiling water. Let boil until the balls float to the surface. Remove with a slotted spoon and place into a basin of iced water to cool.

4. Drain the balls and serve with the syrup.

 Note: The uncooked taro and sweet potato balls can be prepared in advance and kept in the freezer.

2a

2b

2b

DEEP-FRIED SWEET POTATO BALLS

炸地瓜球

Serves 4

Sweet potatoes are to the Taiwanese what potatoes are to the British. The Taiwanese love sweet potato and it is used in both sweet and savoury dishes. These sweet potato balls are very popular as a night market food where they are served sweet. They are simple to make and I make them often at home.

800 g (1³/₄ lb) sweet potatoes, peeled and cut into cubes

90 g (3¹/₄ oz) sugar

240 g (8¹/₂ oz) sweet potato starch

40 g (1¹/₃ oz) white sesame seeds

800 ml (26 fl oz) cooking oil

1. Steam the sweet potatoes until tender, then mash. Mix evenly with the sugar while hot.

2. Add the sweet potato starch and sesame seeds and knead until the mixture is smooth.

3. Pinch off bits of the mixture and roll into ping pong-sized balls.

4. Heat the oil in a wok over medium heat and deep-fry the sweet potato balls in batches. The sweet potato balls are done when they float to the surface. Remove with a slotted spoon. Drain well before serving.

PEANUT AND SESAME MOCHI

花生和芝麻麻糬

Makes 18–20 pieces

Mochi is a dish that is representative of both Taiwan's aboriginal people and the Hakka people. The recipe below is based on Hakka mochi. Hakka mochi is made of glutinous (sticky) rice flour and is coated with peanut or sesame powder and sugar. This is a very simple and tasty dessert, but it must be consumed in moderation as glutinous rice can be very filling and it takes a longer time to digest compared to regular rice.

50 g (1³/₄ oz) blanched peanuts

50 g (1³/₄ oz) black sesame seeds

50 g (1³/₄ oz) white sesame seeds

3 Tbsp castor sugar

Mochi

280 g (10 oz) glutinous rice flour

40 g (1¹/₃ oz) cornflour

50 g (1³/₄ oz) castor sugar

450 ml (15 fl oz) warm water

3 Tbsp vegetable or sunflower oil

1. Preheat the oven to 180°C (350°F). Roast the peanuts for 5–10 minutes until just golden brown. Set aside to cool, then use a food processor to blend the peanuts coarsely. Transfer to a bowl. Roast the black and white sesame seeds for 3–5 minutes separately. Set aside to cool in separate bowls.

2. Add 1 Tbsp castor sugar to each bowl of roasted peanuts and sesame seeds. Mix well and set aside.

3. Prepare the mochi. Place the glutinous rice flour, cornflour, castor sugar and water in a big bowl and mix into a dough. Add the oil and mix evenly.

4. Place the dough in a steamer and steam for 30 minutes. Set aside to cool.

5. Oil your hands and divide the dough into 18–20 equal pieces. Roll into balls.

6. Coat the balls evenly with the peanut or sesame mixture. Serve.

PEANUT PANCAKES 花生麥仔煎

Makes 3 large pancakes

The story behind this snacks goes way back to the Qing Dynasty, when Zuo Zongtang, also known as General Tso, was a Chinese military leader. Once, before he headed out to battle, he asked his chefs to prepare some food that would be easy for the soldiers to carry to the front line. His chefs then created this pancake in the half-moon shape. Despite its military beginnings, these pancakes are absolutely delicious.

Cooking oil, as needed

Peanut Filling
50 g (1³/₄ oz) blanched peanuts
2 Tbsp castor sugar

Pancake Batter
90 g (3¹/₄ oz) plain flour
90 g (3¹/₄ oz) bread flour
¹/₂ tsp bicarbonate of soda
1 tsp baking powder
80 g (2⁴/₅ oz) castor sugar
1 egg
2 Tbsp cooking oil
250 ml (8 fl oz / 1 cup) water

1. Prepare the peanut filling. Preheat the oven to 180°C (350°F). Roast the peanuts for 5–10 minutes until just golden brown. Set aside to cool. Using a food processor, blend the peanuts coarsely, then mix with the sugar. Set aside.

2. Prepare the pancake batter. Sift the plain flour, bread flour, bicarbonate of soda and baking powder into a mixing bowl. Add the sugar, egg, oil and water and use an electric mixer to beat the mixture for 5 minutes. The mixture should be thick and sticky. Set aside.

3. Using a 20–22 cm (7³/₄–8¹/₂ in) round frying pan, heat a little oil over low heat. Add a third of the pancake batter and tilt the pan around so the batter coats the base of the pan evenly. Cover with a lid and let the pancake cook until small bubbles start appearing on the surface of the batter.

4. Spoon a third of the peanut filling over the pancake and fold the pancake in half. Cook both sides of the pancake until golden brown. Remove and set aside.

5. Repeat to make another 2 pancakes.

6. Slice the pancakes and serve.

SWEET GLUTINOUS RICE SOUP WITH DRIED LONGANS AND RED DATES

米糕粥

Serves 4

This is a very old-fashioned Taiwanese dessert, which can be found sold in many night markets in Taiwan. The Taiwanese believe that it is good for health and consuming it in winter will help keep the body warm and prevent colds. It is traditionally served with a little bit of rice wine, but this is entirely optional.

150 g (5^1/$_3$ oz) short-grain glutinous rice

250 ml (8 fl oz / 1 cup) water

Rice wine, to taste (optional)

Soup

250 ml (8 fl oz / 1 cup) + 450 ml (15 fl oz) water

1 Tbsp rock sugar

1 Tbsp dark brown sugar

1 Tbsp dried longans

10 red dates

^{1}/$_2$ tsp salt

Glutinous Rice Flour Slurry

1 Tbsp glutinous rice flour

1^1/$_2$ Tbsp water

1. Rinse the rice and place in a heatproof bowl with the water. Place in a steamer and steam for 30–40 minutes until the rice is cooked and tender.

2. Prepare the soup. Place 250 ml (8 fl oz / 1 cup) water in a saucepan with the rock sugar and dark brown sugar. Bring to a boil, then simmer over low heat for 5 minutes. Set aside.

3. In another saucepan, bring 450 ml (15 fl oz) water, dried longans and red dates to a boil, then simmer over low heat for 15 minutes.

4. Add the cooked rice. Bring to a boil, then simmer over low heat for about 20 minutes until the rice soup looks thick and sticky.

5. Add the syrup and salt and return to the boil.

6. Prepare the glutinous rice flour slurry. Mix the glutinous rice flour with the water and stir into the boiling soup. Cook for another minute and remove from heat.

7. Prepare 4 serving bowls. Add a little rice wine into each bowl if desired, then ladle the rice soup into the bowls. Serve immediately

COFFIN BREAD 棺財板

Serves 4

Coffin bread is a night market snack that originates from Tainan, a city in the South of Taiwan. Coffin bread gets its name from the way the bread is cut to create a box with a lid, resembling a coffin. For this particular recipe, I used a seafood mix with a coating of cheese, but you can use any other filling as well.

40 g (1¹/₃ oz) peas

40 g (1¹/₃ oz) carrot, peeled and cut into pea-size cubes

1¹/₂ Tbsp unsalted butter

40 g (1¹/₃ oz) onion, peeled and finely chopped

2 Tbsp plain flour

300 ml (10 fl oz / 1¹/₄ cups) milk

200 g (7 oz) mixed seafood, such as prawns, squid, mussels, clams and fish

1¹/₂ tsp salt

¹/₄ tsp ground white pepper

1 loaf uncut bread

1 litre (32 fl oz / 4 cups) cooking oil

30 g (1 oz) cheddar cheese or red Leicester, grated

1. Boil a small pot of water and cook the peas until tender. Drain and set aside. Repeat to cook the carrots.

2. Melt the butter in a saucepan over medium heat. Add the onion and stir-fry until soft.

3. Turn to low heat and add the flour. Mix evenly and cook for 20–30 seconds.

4. Add the milk gradually, whisking gently until the mixture is thick and creamy, and there are no lumps.

5. Add the seafood, peas and carrot. Season with salt and pepper. Cook, stirring, to prevent the mixture from burning. Remove from heat when the seafood is done. Set aside.

6. Cut the bread into 4 thick slices, each at least 5-cm (2-in) thick.

7. Heat the oil in a wok to 180°C (350°F) and deep-fry the bread until golden brown and crisp. Drain well.

8. Using a small knife, cut a square out of the top of each piece of bread, then hollow out the bread. Be careful not to cut all the way through the bread.

9. Fill the hollowed-out bread with the seafood and milk sauce and sprinkle the cheese over the sauce.

10. Place the bread under the grill and cook until the cheese is melted.

11. Serve immediately.

FA GAO 發糕

Makes 10–12 pieces

The Chinese name for this steamed cake, *fa gao*, literally means 'raised' cake, but it also means prosperity or promotion in Chinese, hence the Chinese believe that eating this cake will bring good fortune and the opportunity for a promotion.

320 g (11¼ oz) rice flour
100 g (3½ oz) plain flour
15 g (½ oz) baking powder
180 g (6⅓ oz) demerara sugar
50 g (1¾ oz) dark brown sugar
400 ml (13½ fl oz) water

1. Sift the rice flour, plain flour and baking powder into a mixing bowl. Add both types of sugar and mix well. Make a well in the centre of the mixture and add the water. Mix evenly. The batter will be thick and sticky. Let sit for 20 minutes.

2. Place 10–12 small heatproof cups/cupcake moulds in a steamer and steam over high heat for 7–8 minutes until the cups/moulds are warm.

3. Place paper cupcake liners into the cups/moulds and fill until about four-fifths full.

4. Steam for about 30 minutes until the cakes are risen and cooked through.

 Note: Do not open the steamer while the cakes are still steaming as the loss of heat may cause the cakes to fall.

BASIC
STOCKS

UTENSILS

I have provided recipes for some basic stocks which you can use whenever a recipe calls for stock. The stocks will keep refrigerated for up to a week and in the freezer for up to a month. You can also put them in small containers for freezing and thaw only what you need. Although home-made stock does taste better, you can always substitute with stock cubes or ready-made stock from the supermarket if you do not have the time to make the stock from scratch.

VEGETABLE STOCK
Makes about 2 litres (64 fl oz / 8 cups)

200 g (7 oz) onions, peeled and roughly chopped

200 g (7 oz) carrots, peeled and roughly chopped

120 g (4^1/$_3$ oz) leeks, peeled and roughly chopped

120 g (4^1/$_3$ oz) celery, peeled and roughly chopped

2.5 litres (80 fl oz / 10 cups) water

1. Place all the ingredients into a large stockpot. Bring to a boil, then simmer over low heat for 1^1/$_2$ hours. Strain and use as needed.

CHICKEN STOCK
Makes about 2 litres (64 fl oz / 8 cups)

200 g (7 oz) chicken bones

150 g (5^1/$_3$ oz) onion, peeled and roughly chopped

120 g (4^1/$_3$ oz) carrot, peeled and roughly chopped

90 g (3^1/$_4$ oz) celery, roughly chopped

2.5 litres (80 fl oz / 10 cups) water

1. Blanch the chicken bones and rinse under cold water.

2. Place all the ingredients into a large stockpot. Bring to a boil, then simmer over low heat for 2 hours. Skim off any scum that rises to the surface from time to time. Strain and use as needed.

PORK STOCK
Makes about 1.5 litres (48 fl oz / 6 cups)

300 g (11 oz) pork bones

150 g (5^1/$_3$ oz) onion, peeled and roughly chopped

120 g (4^1/$_3$ oz) carrot, peeled and roughly chopped

90 g (3^1/$_4$ oz) celery, roughly chopped

2.5 litres (80 fl oz / 10 cups) water

1. Blanch the pork bones and rinse under cold water.

2. Place all the ingredients into a large stockpot. Bring to a boil, the simmer over low heat for 3–4 hours. Skim off any scum that rises to the surface from time to time. Strain and use as needed.

GLOSSARY

FRESH AND DRIED INGREDIENTS

Bamboo shoot
Bamboo shoot is eaten as a vegetable and it is very popular in Taiwan where it is used in many dishes, from soups and stews to salads and stir-fries. The young shoots of the bamboo plant are harvested in the spring and summer, but sometimes, depending on how warm the seasons are, they can also be harvested during the winter. Bamboo shoots are also pickled and dried for use in cooking.

Glass noodles
These fine translucent noodles are also known as Chinese vermicelli, bean threads and crystal noodles. Glass noodles are sold dried and need to be soaked in warm water to soften before cooking. Glass noodles are bland and take on the flavour of dishes they are used in readily, making them perfect in stir-fries, soups, salads, hotpots and many other kinds of dishes.

Dried longans
Dried longans are popularly used in Taiwanese and Chinese dessert soups to add flavour and sweetness. The Taiwanese also believe that dried longans have many health benefits including improving blood circulation, relieving stress and anxiety, and helping to reduce insomnia. As such, dried longans are popularly used in food therapy and herbal medicines in Taiwan.

Dried prawns (dried shrimps)
Dried prawns, or dried shrimps, are commonly used in Taiwanese cuisine. The small sun-dried prawns have a sweet and unique flavour and taste very different to fresh prawns. They are used to add flavour and texture to many dishes, from soups and braised dishes, to stir-fries and dim sum.

Soak them in warm water to soften before use. As I do not use MSG for cooking, I often use dried prawns as a flavour enhancer. Besides dried prawns, there are also many other types of dried seafood that have the same effect in cooking, including dried scallops, dried squid and dried oysters.

Dried shiitake mushrooms
Dried shiitake mushrooms have a unique earthy aroma and a chewy texture. In Taiwanese cooking, dried shiitake mushrooms feature in many popular dishes from soups, to stews and stir-fries. When shopping for dried shiitake mushrooms, choose whole mushrooms without any broken bits. The mushroom cap should be round, thick and dark brown in colour on the outside and light yellow on the underside. This is where the flavour of shiitake mushrooms come from. Dried shiitake mushrooms need to be soaked in warm water to soften before use.

Dried tangerine peel
This refers to the sun-dried peel of the tangerine fruit. Dried tangerine peel is commonly used in Chinese and Taiwanese cuisine and in herbal medicines. The dried peel has a lovely citrus fragrance and goes well with beef, pork and duck dishes. It is also often added to desserts to enhance the flavour of the dessert.

Dried tofu skin
Also known as bean curd skin, bean curd sheet or bean curd robes, dried tofu skin is made from the skin that forms when soy milk is boiled. These thin sheets of tofu skin are used as edible food wrap. Dried tofu skin is also available in other forms such as sticks and as sweet sheets, and are also commonly used in Chinese cooking.

Pickled cordia

Cordia is also known as clammy cherries, glue berries, sebesten or snotty gobbles. Pickled cordia is a very popular ingredient in Taiwan and is most commonly used in steamed seafood dishes, especially fish dishes. The pickled berries have a salty, sweet and sour flavour. When using pickled cordia in your cooking, bear in mind that other seasoning should be added sparingly.

Pickled melon

Pickled melon is basically Taiwanese-style pickled cucumber. Pickled melon tastes sweet and a little salty. You can use pickled melon to steam fish, to flavour stews and soups and even meatloaf or meatballs.

Preserved chopped radish

Preserved chopped radish is available in packets from markets and supermarkets. It is made from cutting fresh radishes into strips or cubes, then leaving them to sit in salt water before they are pressed and sun-dried. The high salinity means the radishes keep well. Before using, rinse the preserved chopped radish well to remove the excess salt and clean them as the radishes can pick up dirt during the sun-drying process. Preserved chopped radish has a lovely crunchy texture and salty flavour, and is commonly added to soups, main dishes, side dishes and relishes.

Salted duck eggs

Salted duck eggs are made by soaking the eggs in brine, but they were traditionally salted by coating the eggs with a thick layer of salted charcoal paste. In Taiwanese households, salted duck eggs are enjoyed with plain rice soup for their breakfast. As salted duck eggs can be very salty, dishes using the eggs should not be over seasoned. The egg yolks from salted duck eggs are a key ingredient in Chinese mooncakes and other Chinese and Taiwanese desserts.

Waxed pork / New Year pork

This cured meat or sun-dried marinated pork is a must-have ingredient for the Chinese New Year. It can be described as a Chinese version of Italian pancetta as it has a smoky, salty flavour not unlike pancetta. Waxed pork is used in many different kinds of dishes, from stir-fries to soups and stews, and it goes well with vegetables like cabbage and leek.

FLOURS

Glutinous rice flour

This fine white flour is commonly used for making desserts in both Taiwanese and Chinese cuisine. It is made from ground glutinous (sticky) rice and is the main ingredient for mochi and *tang yuan*, giving these desserts a lovely chewy texture. Glutinous rice flour is not the same as rice flour and cannot be used interchangeably.

Potato starch

Made from potatoes, this white flour is typically used to thicken sauces and soups and to marinate meat in Chinese and Taiwanese cuisine, much like cornflour. Cornflour can be used if potato starch is not available.

Sweet potato flour
An extract of white sweet potatoes, sweet potato flour has a sweet flavour and is used in Chinese and Taiwanese cooking as a coating for deep-fried foods, desserts and soups.

Tapioca flour
Tapioca flour is extracted from the tapioca root. It is commonly used in making desserts in Taiwan and is perhaps most popularly used in drinks like pearl milk tea (also known as Bubble Tea) where it is a main ingredient for the chewy tapioca pearls.

HERBS AND SPICES

Chinese angelica root
Also known as *dong quai*, this root of the Angelica sinensis is commonly used in herbal medicines, but can also be used as a spice in cooking, such as in the Taiwanese dish, drunken chicken. It is believed that the Chinese angelica root can help to improve blood circulation.

Chinese five-spice powder
Chinese five-spice powder is commonly made from a combination of five spices, namely star anise, cloves, Chinese cinnamon (cassia), Sichuan peppercorns and fennel seeds. In Chinese and Taiwanese cooking, five-spice powder is used when cooking fatty meats like pork and for flavouring stews.

Licorice root
Licorice comes from the root of the Glycyrrhiza glabra plant. It has a natural, earthy and mellow sweet flavour and is used in herbal medicines, cooking and sweets. Both Chinese and Taiwanese cuisine use licorice root as a spice. It helps balance the flavour of other spices used and gives the dish a natural and subtle sweetness.

Sichuan peppercorns
One of the spices in Chinese five-spice powder, Sichuan peppercorns have very strong flavour with a powerful, numbing taste. Its heat can be likened to that of very strong chillies and it can be added to give a lift to sauces and dressings.

Wolfberries
Also known as goji or goji berries, wolfberries are commonly used in herbal medicine and as a cooking spice. The Chinese also refer to them as "red diamond fruit" for their many health benefits. Dried wolfberries can be used in soups, stews and stir-fries to add a sweet flavour to the dish. They can also be added to herbal teas.

OILS, SAUCES AND PASTES

Black vinegar
Black vinegar is made from glutinous rice and has a rich, mellow and sweet flavour. The best black vinegar is said to be from Zhenjiang in China. In my opinion, black vinegar is less pungent than rice vinegar and is more fragrant. Black vinegar can be used as an ingredient in cooking and as a condiment.

Chilli bean sauce
Chilli bean sauce has been called the soul of Sichuan cuisine, being the main seasoning ingredient for many popular Sichuan dishes. Also known as *dou ban jiang*, this rich, brown-coloured paste is made from fermented broad beans, soy beans, salt, rice and spices, and is a combination of spicy and salty flavours.

Dark sesame oil and sesame oil

Sesame oil is a popular ingredient in Taiwanese cooking and it is used in many different dishes including soups, noodles and rice dishes. Dark sesame oil is derived from toasted or roasted sesame seeds. It has a stronger flavour compared to regular sesame oil and is hence not as popular as the latter. It is mainly used in the Taiwanese three-cup dishes and sesame chicken soup. In Taiwan, it is also used in preparing confinement food as it is believed that sesame oil helps the womb contract, increases blood circulation and warms the body.

Oyster sauce

Traditionally, oyster sauce was made by simmering oysters in water until the juices caramelised into a thick, brown and intensely flavourful sauce. However, oyster sauce is now typically made with a base of sugar and salt thickened with cornflour. Oyster sauce can be used as both a seasoning and marinade for meat and vegetable dishes.

Pineapple bean sauce

Pineapple bean sauce is a product unique to Taiwan. It is sold in jars and is available from supermarkets specialising in Taiwanese food products. Pineapple bean sauce is a combination of salt, fermented beans, sugar and pickled pineapple, and tastes both sweet and salty. Dishes flavoured with pineapple bean sauce do not require additional seasoning.

Red vinasse (red wine lees)

Red vinasse is the fermented rice left over after making Fuzhou red wine. It is also known as red yeast rice or red fermented rice. Marinating meat with this sauce gives the meat a slight fragrance of rice wine. Red vinasse has a unique taste and even if you do not like rice wine, you may still take a liking to this.

Rice wine and Shaoxing rice wine

Rice wine and Shaoxing rice wine are the two common types of rice wine used in Chinese and Taiwanese cooking. They are sold in bottles and are available in supermarkets and Chinese grocery stores. Rice wine (米酒) is made from regular rice and is colourless. Shaoxing rice wine (紹興酒) is made from glutinous rice and is usually brown in colour. Shaoxing rice wine has a much stronger flavour and taste of alcohol and is also a little spicy, which makes it unsuitable for many dishes, except for stronger tasting dishes such as drunken chicken, drunken prawns, Dongpo pork and other slow-cooked meat dishes. Rice wine on the other hand has a mild and refreshing taste and I use it to season many Chinese and Taiwanese dishes.

Soy sauce

There are many different types of soy sauce, and the most common types are dark soy sauce, light soy sauce and thick soy sauce. Dark soy sauce is typically used to add colour to dishes. Light soy sauce is most commonly used as a marinade, seasoning and condiment. Light soy sauce can be very salty, so use sparingly. As its name implies, thick soy sauce has a thick texture, somewhat like honey and it is both sweet and salty. It is often used to flavour stews and sauces, and can also be used as a dip.

PLUM PEELED TOMATOES
IN TOMATO JUICE

WEIGHTS AND MEASURES

Quantities for this book are given in Metric and American (spoon and cup) measures. Standard spoon and cup measurements used are: 1 teaspoon = 5 ml, 1 tablespoon = 15 ml and 1 cup = 250 ml. All measures are level unless otherwise stated.

LIQUID AND VOLUME MEASURES

Metric	Imperial	American
5 ml	$^1/_6$ fl oz	1 teaspoon
10 ml	$^1/_3$ fl oz	1 dessertspoon
15 ml	$^1/_2$ fl oz	1 tablespoon
60 ml	2 fl oz	$^1/_4$ cup (4 tablespoons)
85 ml	$2^1/_2$ fl oz	$^1/_3$ cup
90 ml	3 fl oz	$^3/_8$ cup (6 tablespoons)
125 ml	4 fl oz	$^1/_2$ cup
180 ml	6 fl oz	$^3/_4$ cup
250 ml	8 fl oz	1 cup
300 ml	10 fl oz ($^1/_2$ pint)	$1^1/_4$ cups
375 ml	12 fl oz	$1^1/_2$ cups
435 ml	14 fl oz	$1^3/_4$ cups
500 ml	16 fl oz	2 cups
625 ml	20 fl oz (1 pint)	$2^1/_2$ cups
750 ml	24 fl oz ($1^1/_5$ pints)	3 cups
1 litre	32 fl oz ($1^3/_5$ pints)	4 cups
1.25 litres	40 fl oz (2 pints)	5 cups
1.5 litres	48 fl oz ($2^2/_5$ pints)	6 cups
2.5 litres	80 fl oz (4 pints)	10 cups

DRY MEASURES

Metric	Imperial
30 grams	1 ounce
45 grams	$1^1/_2$ ounces
55 grams	2 ounces
70 grams	$2^1/_2$ ounces
85 grams	3 ounces
100 grams	$3^1/_2$ ounces
110 grams	4 ounces
125 grams	$4^1/_2$ ounces
140 grams	5 ounces
280 grams	10 ounces
450 grams	16 ounces (1 pound)
500 grams	1 pound, $1^1/_2$ ounces
700 grams	$1^1/_2$ pounds
800 grams	$1^3/_4$ pounds
1 kilogram	2 pounds, 3 ounces
1.5 kilograms	3 pounds, $4^1/_2$ ounces
2 kilograms	4 pounds, 6 ounces

OVEN TEMPERATURE

	°C	°F	Gas Regulo
Very slow	120	250	1
Slow	150	300	2
Moderately slow	160	325	3
Moderate	180	350	4
Moderately hot	190/200	370/400	5/6
Hot	210/220	410/440	6/7
Very hot	230	450	8
Super hot	250/290	475/550	9/10

LENGTH

Metric	Imperial
0.5 cm	$^1/_4$ inch
1 cm	$^1/_2$ inch
1.5 cm	$^3/_4$ inch
2.5 cm	1 inch